Elizabeth,

You are a Princess! Make sure you are always treated like one.

Happy Valentines Day!

Sylvia Carvajal ♡♡

Men Are PIGS!

Outrageous Stories from Women About Men's Bad Behavoir

Sylvia Carvajal

ROOFTOP
publishing

Rooftop Publishing™
1663 Liberty Drive, Suite 200
Bloomington, IN 47403
Phone: 1-800-839-8640

This book is a work of non-fiction. Unless otherwise noted, the author and the publisher make no explicit guarantees as to the accuracy of the information contained in this book and in some cases, names of people and places have been altered to protect their privacy.

©2006 Sylvia Carvajal. All rights reserved

No part of this book may be reproduced, stored in a retrieval system, or transmitted by any means without the written permission of the author.

First published by Rooftop Publishing 10/13/2006

ISBN: 1-60008-016-2 (sc)

Printed in the United States of America
Bloomington, Indiana

This book is printed on acid-free paper.

Dedication

Ken, you are the love of my life and the man of my dreams. Thank you for accepting the way I am and for encouraging me to be myself. Thank you for your love and understanding, especially as I completed this book. I love, love, love you always!

Acknowledgments

To Lisa Michelle, my beautiful and wonderful little girl: Thank you for the unconditional love you have given me during the first eleven years of your life. Thank you for letting me be the mom. My waking thoughts are of you. My last thoughts are of you as I lay my head to sleep. There are moments we share that I would love to freeze forever. Thank you for keeping me grounded. Yes, my life would have been different without you. However, my life is so wonderfully better because of you.

Raising a child as a single parent has been the greatest challenge I have ever faced ... Wait a minute. I'm married! Seriously, I can fully appreciate the struggles my parents faced when I was growing up. My mother was lucky because my father is the greatest human being in the entire world. Together with their individual, yet complementary, senses of humor, my parents raised three children.

To Antonia Garza, my mother in every sense of the word: Thank you for sharing your wisdom and for being my greatest source of love and encouragement.

To Baldemar Garza, my father: Thank you for always being my daddy. Thank you for setting the example for the kind of man I always wanted to marry. Dad, you and I share a bond that few people will ever experience. Remember, I am the good daughter.

To Yolanda Morales, my favorite sister—okay, my only sister: You are everything a big sister should be. Sis, thank you for always taking care of me. Thank you for sticking up for me and always taking my side. Thank you for your encouraging words. You always know what to say when my life is crashing in around me. I carry with me the knowledge that if anything ever happens to me, you will help raise my daughter. I have no greater comfort.

To Joby Garza, my baby brother: Even though you are my little brother, you always know when to act like a big brother. Thank you for being so supportive and generous with me. Thank you for not getting mad at me about blowing the engine in your truck. I can always count on you when I need anything.

To Steven Cords, my friend and confidant: Thank you for staying my friend even though we are a million miles apart. Thank you for sharing your bright and intelligent humor. Thank you for sharing your thoughts as I wrote this book. I took to heart the sound advice you gave me. I hope you recognize your contributions.

I want to thank all my girlfriends who shared their stories and experiences. I want to recognize the women I spoke with, some of them strangers, who shared their experiences. I want to express my sincere appreciation to all of you because when you acknowledged that you had a pig in your life, you had to face reality. Some of your stories and experiences were nothing to laugh about. The stories conveyed your incredible courage and strength. Bouquets of flowers to all of you! I have included some of your stories. To protect your privacy, I did not use your real names. In most instances, only you will recognize your story.

When I started writing this book, I wanted to cover a variety of topics and issues that women face in their relationships with men. My goal was to make you smile and, in some instances, to make you laugh out loud. My hope is to remind you that you are not alone. Always remember, you can always count on your girlfriends, your sisters, your mothers, and your daughters.

Preface

As a first-time author, I was completely unprepared for how people reacted to the book and what they had to say about it. The title, in and of itself, was enough to evoke a slew of verbal and non-verbal reactions. It was no surprise that almost all of the women who read the title for the first time simultaneously laughed and, in one manner or another, agreed. The reactions to the book from women were actually very similar. I received numerous unsolicited emails and telephone calls from women after they read the book. Most of the comments were simple like, "I just read your book. I wish I had read it three marriages ago." I loved the comments, which included, "I read your book in one night. I couldn't put it down." What most amazed me was how many women felt compelled to share their stories with me. They all seemed to start the same way: "You should hear my story." I heard so many horrible stories. The stories were so depressing that they started to affect me both physically and emotionally. However, the stories also validated my work, and most especially, the title of the book.

I can recall at least three women who did not approve of the "Men Are Pigs" part of the title. I was somewhat surprised at the manner in which they defended men and either admonished me or called me names such as "feminist," "male basher," and "man hater." I prefer "Princess"! One woman, with her husband in tow, walked up to me at a book signing and told me that if a woman learned to be loving and submissive to a man, he would do anything to make her happy and treat her like a queen. Biting my lip, I fought back the urge to tell her that it must be nice living in her delusional little world. Instead, I said, "No hablo ingles."

As far as the men's reactions to the title of the book, let me just say that most of them were less than supportive. Some were quite offensive. After all, men are pigs! However, there were a number of men who laughed at the title. Some just admitted, "I'm a pig," or "Most of my friends are pigs." Other men did not seem offended in the least. Most of these men offered examples to prove they were good guys. For the most part, I believed them. I was ready to bring them home. But then, I'd have a lot of explaining to do. Sometimes, my husband does not have a sense of humor.

Introduction

My parents always seemed to be in love. Even now, they hold hands when they walk together. My father is seventy-five years old, and my mother is seventy-one years old. I never worried that they might divorce. They never did. When I was growing up, I thought every man was like my father. He was a family man in every sense of the word. My parents had three children. I am the middle child. When we were babies, our father changed our diapers, helped with our feedings, and helped to take care of us. Cold mornings always kept us underneath the blankets. My father would iron our clothes and then toss them under our blankets so that we could put on our clothes while they were still warm. It made it easier to get out of bed.

I do not remember my father raising his voice at us and certainly not at my mother. I never saw my parents fight or argue. I imagine that they had their quarrels, but they did not quarrel in front of us. My father's motto was very simple: "Ask your mother; whatever she says."

Once, at a family reunion, my uncle was telling a story about his relationship with his wife. His point was that he only had to strike her once to put her in her place. My father, who was stretched out on a lounge chair, did not say anything, but he shook his head in disagreement. My uncle caught my father's gesture and, in front of everyone, asked my father, "Can you honestly tell us that you have never hit your wife?"

My father said, "Are you serious? She'll beat the shit out of me." Everyone started laughing. I think it was because they all knew it was probably true.

My father enjoyed an occasional beer, but I never saw him drunk. He did not smoke. He never went drinking with "the guys" after work. On occasion, he went to bachelor parties and retirement parties. He was always home early. For the most part, he came straight home from work, helped with dinner, and if it was my turn, helped me wash the dishes. Since my parents both worked, there was a division of labor at home. My mother was not killing herself while my father sat on the couch and watched television. My cousin Angie once asked my father why he was always so good about helping with the cooking and the cleaning. My father told her that if he helped my mother, she would not be too tired to spend time with him. Smart man, huh?

My mother helped my sister, my brother, and me with schoolwork and school projects. I was once a grammar book in a school play. My mother spent hours helping me memorize my lines until I had memorized the entire school play. That came in handy when one of the other "books" got the mumps, and the alternate had not memorized her lines.

As we were growing up, we participated in sports: baseball, track, gymnastics, drill team, and cheerleading. My father helped with our practices, and my mother made sure we had the equipment and clothes that we needed. They both went to all of our games and events. Every summer, my parents bought us season passes for the community swimming pool. We went swimming almost every day. For hours, my mother sat on the shaded bleachers talking with the other mothers. She never complained.

Almost every Saturday morning, my father played golf with his friends. He left the house before we were awake. He was usually home before noon. The reason he was home before noon was that he knew my mother wanted to spend the afternoon with him. They always went shopping together. They would often take drives to the beach or to visit relatives and friends. On most Saturday nights, they went dancing. My parents would get all dressed up. They acted like they were still dating. My father was usually dressed before my mother, way before. After splashing on cologne, he would walk into the living room and patiently wait for her. I always said to him, "Dad, you look good."

He would respond, as he checked himself out in the mirror, "No, I look great!"

One evening, we all went to a wedding reception. My parents were sitting at a long table. The women were sitting on one side of the table, and the men were sitting on the other side of the table, opposite their wives. Some of the men were having a conversation at the end of the table. A woman, whose husband was involved in the conversation, was dancing next to the table by herself. She stopped dancing and came up behind my father and put her hands on his shoulders. Even from where I was standing, I could see she was pressing her breasts against my father's back.

She looked over my father's shoulder at my mother and asked her, "You don't mind if I dance with your husband, do you?"

My mother said, "Of course not, go ahead." Then my mother said to my father, "She wants to dance with you."

My sister and I stopped what we were doing and watched in horror. We held our breaths and waited. But my father did not move.

The woman nudged him and said, "Come on, let's dance."

He still did not move. When she nudged him again, my father said, "I don't want to dance."

The woman said teasingly, "Oh come on, just one dance."

My father then said, "No, I only dance with my wife."

The woman seemed a bit embarrassed. She continued dancing alone next to the table before dancing away. My sister and I breathed a sigh of relief. We did not want any other woman dancing with our father. We did not understand why our mother had urged our father to dance with that woman. She was obviously flirting with our dad.

When we got home, my sister asked my mother why she had told my father that he could dance with the woman. My mother said, "Your father knew better than to get up. Permission or no permission, your dad would have never danced with her."

My parents have a great relationship. If you ask my father, he'll tell you that my mother always comes first. I have always believed that my father loves my mother more than she loves him. Oh, she loves him. He just loves her more. One day, we came home from the funeral of a close family friend. The man had died of a sudden heart attack. His wife and children, who were held together by the love and devotion of this man, were falling apart. It was heartbreaking. That evening, during dinner with my parents, my sister, my brother, and I ate quietly.

My father suddenly said, "If your mother dies before I do, you guys might as well wait and bury us together because I do not want to live without her."

Before any of us had a chance to respond, my mother said, "Well, if your father dies before I do, I'm getting married again."

My father put his fork down and crossed his arms. He pouted until my mother reassured him she was just joking. She kissed him over and over until he got over it. It is a moment I will cherish forever. That was true love, and I wanted my life to turn out like that.

The truth is that I wanted to be Cinderella. I wanted the beautiful gown with the matching crown and the glass slippers. I could have endured the abuse from the wicked step-monster and the two wicked stepsisters. I would have cleaned and washed and cooked. I would have slept next to the chimney. I would have gone through anything because one day I would meet my handsome prince. He would fall in love with me and take me to his castle. I would always be happy because I would want for nothing. There would always be sunshine in my days. Moonlit skies with bright stars would fill my nights. I would have the perfect life. I would have perfect children. I would be beautiful forever. My husband would be beautiful, and my children would be beautiful. And I would live happily ever after … WAKE UP!

I spent an enormous amount of time asking women what they considered to be the most important issues they faced in their relationships with men. Drawing on those issues, I was able to write the following chapters. I believe that most women will be able to relate, or will know someone who can relate, to what I have written in one or more of these chapters. The only issue that I chose not to write about in any great detail is domestic abuse, although there is some brief discussion about domestic abuse in one chapter. This was too painful an issue, and there is nothing funny about domestic abuse.

If you are ready to begin your journey, find a nice quiet spot, kick off your shoes, and put your feet up. The next person that bothers you, tell him or her, "You see this book? It means that I'm trying to read. So, go make yourself a sandwich, find whatever it is you've misplaced, and sex is out of the question until you apologize." Then, with the wave of one hand, whisper, "Go away."

Contents

1. Men Are Pigs! 1
2. The Gauge 7
3. I Can Kill My Own Spiders 33
4. The Worst Thing About Motherhood… 37
5. I Am, Therefore I Shop 45
6. When Intelligent Men Say Stupid Things 51
7. A Woman Scorned 61
8. Today Is Our What? 69
9. Guy@homewatchingsports.com 75
10. Sexhausted 81
11. Say It with Me: Laundry 85
12. If I Had a Wife Instead of a Husband… 91
13. Recipe for a Great Fruit Salad 95
14. Incredible Weight-loss Program 103
15. Princess Power 109
16. I Once Discovered the Secret to a Perfect Marriage, but I Forgot to Write It Down 119

1.

Men Are Pigs!

A woman was walking along the beach when she came upon a beautiful bottle partially buried in the sand. She picked it up, and as she pulled out the cork, a genie appeared before her eyes.

The genie said, "I will grant you one wish."

The woman thought about wishing for fame or fortune. She thought about wishing for eternal life. But she quickly realized that this was one shot to wish for something great. She walked with the genie to her car and pulled out a map. Pointing to the countries in the Middle East, she told the genie, "I want peace in the Middle East," she said. "I want these countries to stop fighting. I want the Arabs to love the Jews and the Jews to love the Arabs. I want Syria, Iran, and Iraq to stop hating the Americans. That is what I wish for."

The genie looked at the map and said, "I do not have the power to do that. These countries have been at war for thousands of years. It cannot be done. I'm sorry. You will have to make another wish."

Disappointed, the woman thought for a moment and said, "Well, I've never been able to find the right man. I want a man who is sensitive and understanding. I want a man who is fun and who gets along with my family and my friends. I want a man who will help with the house cleaning. I don't want him watching sports all the time, and he has to be faithful."

The genie looked at her for a moment and then said, "Let me see that map again."

—Unknown

Okay, so men are pigs. But why? Are men and women that different? The answer is yes. We are very different. Our physical differences are quite obvious, but our psychological differences are not so obvious. During the initial phases of our relationships with men, we are not as astute to these differences. We are intoxicated with love. However, as the relationship progresses, we wake up to a serious hangover. We struggle to maintain the relationship, as we are faced with a great deal of frustration and anger over their "man/pig" behavior. It seems that men can be good only for short periods of time. Mostly, they act like total pigs. It is no small wonder that women become resentful and unforgiving, even bitter. And it takes a long time to achieve bitterness. Sure, it's a good excuse to say that we are different. Men use this excuse, as needed, so they do not have to be held accountable for their actions.

Relationships between men and women are complex, but they don't have to be. We can either choose to be good to each other or not. We either want the relationship to work or not. It is that simple. When men want to be nice, they can be nice. When men want to be helpful, they can be helpful. When men want sex, they are nice. When they want sex, they are helpful. Otherwise, they are just men acting like pigs.

Men's behavior that women find so frustrating and annoying is not difficult to describe. Men just do a lot of things that make women angry. They also do not do a lot of things that make women angry. When I asked women to tell me what it was that bugged them about men, most of the women needed about a day and a half. I did not have that kind of time, but I needed to make a list of these statements. So, I took a sheet of paper and on the left side of the page, I wrote: "MEN: PROS." On the right side of the page, I wrote: "MEN: CONS." I made a bunch of copies, and then I asked my girlfriends to list what they disliked about men and to list what they liked about men.

The first list I got back was from Diana. She had more than thirty entries under cons. The left side of the page was blank.

I said, "You forgot to make a list of the pros."

She chuckled and then said, "No, I didn't. I couldn't think of anything."

When Julie gave me her list, I noticed that she, too, had nothing listed on the pros side. When I asked her where her list of pros was, she said, "Oh, I thought you were kidding."

She took the list back and went to work on the pros side of the page. She brought the list back ten minutes later. She had listed two pros. And so it went. There were one or two pros and long lists of cons.

Check out the list of the cons below. Although I collected more than two hundred entries, there were a number that were of the "scum-sucking, pig bastards" type. I had to draw the line somewhere. I chose only the following. I did not list the pros because they were too few and insignificant. No surprise, huh? Read on:

1. Men lie and cheat, and then they lie about lying and lie about cheating.
2. Men don't help with housework.
3. Men give you the silent treatment as punishment.
4. Men burp and fart, and they think it's funny.
5. Men won't take care of their kids.
6. Men will treat their friends better than they treat you.
7. Men will continuously watch sports, sports, and more sports.
8. Men never listen.
9. Men are hurtful and never apologize.
10. Men will ignore you and not take your calls.
11. Men take no interest in anything we do.
12. Men refuse to put the toilet seat down.
13. Men are insensitive and uncaring.
14. Men prefer to be with their friends.
15. Men say they love you, but they never show it.
16. Men are lazy.
17. Men forget birthdays and anniversaries.
18. Men make dates, but they forget to show up.

19. Men don't care if we are sick.
20. Men do not buy flowers or gifts.
21. Men won't give backrubs or foot massages.
22. Men treat women like garbage.
23. Men think nothing of showing up two hours late for a date.
24. Men never take the blame for anything.
25. Men will make promises, which they always break.

Now read them again. This time add, "unless they want sex." It's no secret. Men will do just about anything upon the promise of sex. Women know that sex is their best bargaining tool. Women can usually get anything they want if they promise sex. Men cannot use sex to get what they want because sex is what they want ... thus, no bargaining tool. If men could only learn that they can get anything they want in exchange for snuggling or a nice foot massage.

I discovered that many women found it embarrassing to share what men had put them through, not to mention what they had allowed men to get away with. Some women had a difficult time saying anything bad about their husbands or boyfriends. However, they had no problem sharing very private and intimate details about their ex-husbands and ex-boyfriends. Once women got through the first sentence, the rest of the story just poured out. Each story was worse than the last, like these women were trying to win a Bad Husband contest. I got a lot of "My ex-husband once ..." or "My friend has a husband who ..." or "That's nothing. I have a friend whose husband ..." Women typically expressed anger when sharing stories. I can only imagine how furious they must have been at the time. Remarkably, there were stories that contained some element of humor. Finding humor in the worst of circumstances made it easier to live with and accept these men. Otherwise, there would be a lot of dead boyfriends and husbands.

I know now that to express anger meant these women would have to confront their primary emotion, and that was hurt. For some women, the memories and their experiences with men were just too painful. I talked to women who had been hurt or mistreated by every man they had ever known. In some instances, women had been hurt or mistreated by the same men for years. Still, the women usually made excuses for these men. Over and over, I heard, "I know he loves me," and "He is not always like that," or "He is a good husband, boyfriend, etc."

An interesting thing that I found was that none of the women I talked to ever said, "It's my fault." None of the women believed that they had done anything to deserve the way they were treated by men. In fact, most of the women expressed just how hard they worked on improving and maintaining their relationships with men. Most of the women also expressed great unhappiness in their relationships. They felt unloved, and they were emotionally exhausted. Most of all, they were unable to communicate this to men, who were uncaring and indifferent anyway. Most of the women had once believed that if they were better wives, better lovers, better mothers, better providers, etc., their husbands would appreciate them more. That did not happen.

Mary said, "I tried everything. I quit nagging Jake about not helping around the house. I stopped asking him to help with the children. I initiated sex, even when I was tired and not in the mood. I stopped arguing with him. I stopped saying anything when he came home late, even on the weekends. I stopped bringing up the fact that he spent more time with his friends than he did with his family. I even ignored the lipstick I found smeared on one of his shirts. I knew that I had not smeared the lipstick on his shirt. I knew because the lipstick shade was one I did not use. I also knew because we no longer hugged or snuggled. Sex was sex. It was the only time he would say that he missed me. Once in a great while, he said he loved me, but only during sex. I moved out the weekend he said he was going hunting with his friends, Nick and Danny. I knew all of his friends, and he didn't have any friends named Nick and Danny."

Mary continued, "I took two boxes of bullets to his rifle and hid them in my closet. Jake went through the motions of packing for the hunting trip. He never asked me about the bullets. He also forgot to take a number of items he would have needed for a hunting trip, including his binoculars and a sleeping bag. He didn't even take his rifle. When I asked him if he was taking his rifle, he stumbled over his words. He managed to say that it was at Nick's house and that Nick would bring it for him. I knew that Jake would have never left his rifle at anyone's house, not ever. When I asked him why he was taking his cologne and shaving kit, he said he wanted to be clean for me when he came home. He made an attempt to sound sincere, but it was lame.

"I started packing as soon as he walked out the door. Before I left the house, I put the two boxes of bullets on the kitchen counter. I found the rifle, which he had hidden in the garage. I positioned the rifle on a chair with the barrel pointing directly at the front door. I wanted Jake to be staring down the barrel of his rifle when he came through the front door. Then, I drove away and I never came back. The only thing I regret is not being there to see the look on his face when he walked through the door."

When a woman decides to leave her husband, she has done everything she can to make the relationship work. She is at the point of emotional exhaustion. She is no longer willing to endure the neglect. She is no longer willing to endure the constant criticism. She is no longer willing to endure any type of abuse. She harbors a deep dissatisfaction with the relationship. By the same token, she cannot understand why her husband will do little, or nothing, to help resolve any of the problems in their marriage. Oblivious to the needs of his wife, a husband can only ask, "What did I do?"

A great number of men have problems and issues that keep them from developing healthy relationships with women. By the time a woman discovers the nature of these problems and issues, she may already be deeply involved in the relationship. She may not know how to end the relationship. She may also hope that, with her love, support, and patience, he will eventually change. Fat chance! Men do not change—ever! If you do not like X, Y, and Z about him, and you decide to stay with him anyway, be prepared for a disappointing and miserable relationship. It will not get better, and you know that.

2.

The Gauge

A man and a woman met at a bar. They talked all night long, and they found they had a lot in common. They ordered round after round of drinks. When the bar closed, the woman invited the man over for a nightcap. At her apartment, one thing led to another, and they found themselves naked and in her bed. At the "moment of truth," the woman, who was lying on her back, looked up at the man.

Sheepishly, she said to the man, "Wait ... I need to know something."
"What?" the man asked.
She asked, "Are you going to respect me in the morning?"
Frustrated, the man answered, "I'm not going to be here in the morning."

—*Unknown*

I knew my husband for three years before we dated. We were both members at a local health club. The first time I saw him was at the racquetball courts. I was sitting on a chair, changing into my court shoes. I saw him come through the door, and I just about fell out of my chair. He was unbelievably gorgeous. He had a boyish haircut and a perfectly symmetrical face. Actually, he looked like Montgomery Cliff when he appeared in the movie *A Place in the Sun*, except in color. He took my breath away. He seemed very sweet. He was friendly, but he was very shy.

For a long time, all I knew about him was his first name, Ken. I loved that name. Some of the racquetball players called him Kenny. I later found out that his nieces and nephews called him Kenneth. His mother called him Kenneth Dean. It was a cool name for a cool guy. Everybody at the racquetball courts knew who he was. All I knew was that the world seemed brighter.

We were always friendly to each other. Sometimes, if we needed an extra player, the girls and I would make Ken play, only left-handed. One day, I saw him reading a book outside of the racquetball courts. I went over and plopped myself next to him.

"What are you reading?" I asked him.

He told me, but I don't remember. I didn't care what he was reading. I just wanted to sit next to him. He said I could borrow the book when he was done reading it.

I said, "I'd like that." I told him I would bring him one of my favorite books in exchange. And so it went.

Next to the health club was a nightclub, and Thursday night was Country Night. My girlfriends and I had agreed we would go dancing that night. We agreed to meet at the health club. As I walked inside the health club, Ken was just leaving. His white T-shirt was soaking wet. Thirteen years later, I still remember that ... vividly. He stopped to talk to me and asked me where I was going. I was not wearing my workout clothes, so it was obvious I was not there to work out. I told him I was meeting my girlfriends because we were going dancing next door.

He softly said, "I want to come."

So I said, "Well, go home and get dressed."

He said he would be back in an hour and walked out the door.

I hesitated and then followed him out and asked him, "Do you dance?"

As he got on his motorcycle, he looked at me, smiled, and nodded.

To this day, that night is one of the most memorable nights Ken and I ever had together. We danced all night long. The night was absolutely perfect! At some point, I gave him my telephone number. He said he would call. On Saturday night, I went out with one of my girlfriends. We stayed out very late. When I got home, I noticed that there were seven messages on my answering machine. I played them back, and all seven were from Ken. Since it was late, I did not think it was a good idea to call him back. I was still contemplating my next move when the telephone rang. It was Ken! He wanted to know if he could come over because he had something very important to tell me. I reluctantly agreed and gave him directions to my house. Forty-five minutes later, I was still waiting for him, and I was getting annoyed. When he finally showed up, he had a dozen roses in one hand and a popular women's magazine in the other hand. Instead of saying, "You are late," I thought, "You are so forgiven."

After some small talk, he told me he wanted me to sit on the couch because he had something he wanted to tell me. First, he made me promise not to laugh. I promised, of course. He paced back and forth a few times and then he stopped and looked right at me.

In a serious voice, he said, "I am in love with you. I've been in love with you for the past six months. You can ask my friend Rob. I want to marry you, and I want for us to have a baby together."

A laugh escaped me. It was out before I could cover my mouth. Ken then hit (tapped) me over the head. I did not know what to say. All I knew was that I had to marry this man. Yes, I would marry this man and I would have his baby. She would be a beautiful baby, and she would look just like him. Did I mention I wanted to be Cinderella?

This guy was truly in love with me. He would call and leave messages that said, "It's Ken. Call me back at 686-L*O*V*E." How adorable is that? He bought me lots of gifts, although some of them were a bit unconventional. One time, he bought me a bronze statue of a man on a horse being attacked by a buffalo. I did not know where to put it in my home because it just did not go with my "princess" motif.

One day, he bought me a set of golf clubs. However, I didn't know how to play golf. I proceeded to take all of the golf clubs out of the golf bag. I took out the golf video that was in one of the zippered pockets, along with a bag of tees.

He finally asked, "What are you looking for?"

I said, "I'm looking for my engagement ring."

He laughed and said, "This IS your engagement ring. It's my commitment to you. I'm going to take you to the golf course with me."

Another time, he bought me a black and hot pink wet suit. It was a size 4, but it looked like a size 2.

He held it up and said, "Try it on."

I tried to put it on, but it kept sticking to my skin. I thought, "Baby powder."

I took it off, dusted my body with baby powder, and tried again. This time it fit, but I couldn't breathe. I was still thinking of where I could possibly wear this thing. It's not like you can wear shoes with a wet suit. You have to wear flippers, and flippers are not exactly shoes. I finally understood that the wet suit was so that we could go scuba diving and snorkeling together. While I found his gesture terribly romantic, I found it equally terrifying. Somehow, I had forgotten to mention to him that I had an extreme and unreasonable fear of water, and underwater caves, and sharks, and artificial breathing apparatuses, and last but not least, drowning. Of course, I promised to take diving classes. When I did not go, I promised that if he took me to Hawaii, I would take diving classes. When he agreed to take me to Hawaii, I promised to go with him on the boat to make sandwiches and serve drinks. Then, I remembered that I get seasick.

Ken was quite charming. He was a dream come true. This kind of stuff did not happen to me, and it had never happened to anyone I knew. I had a list of dating nightmares along with the monsters that were in those nightmares. This guy was different. I could feel a fairytale coming on. I had found my prince! Have I mentioned that I wanted to be Cinderella?

You might wonder, "Was he that perfect?" To answer that question, I must first ask you to mark this page, close the book, and read the title again. So, I guess the answer is, "Not entirely." Still, he was close, and I was keeping this one. I found myself insanely in love with him.

My scenario is quite the exception. The ugly reality is that dating is tough at any age. The toughest part is finding someone you actually want to date. When we are young, we are so idealistic about love. We do believe that we live happily ever after. All of our childhood stories tell us that. Even the movies that we watch plant that crap in our minds. Of course, we believe it because we want it to be true. That is the way love is supposed to be.

I was once talking to a small group of young girls. With the exception of Melissa, a twenty-four-year-old beauty, who was married with two toddlers, the girls ranged in ages from twelve through sixteen.

As Melissa left the room to get a drink from the kitchen, one of the girls asked, "Do guys ever fall in love?"

"Yes," I answered.

Then another girl asked, "Do guys just want one thing?"

"Yes," I acknowledged.

"All the time?" one of the girls asked.

"Yes," I answered firmly.

Melissa returned to the room and sat on the floor. Pointing to Melissa, I said to the girls, "If you don't believe me, let's ask her."

I asked Melissa, "What do all guys want?"

Without hesitation, she said, "Sex."

I asked her, "Every guy?"

She said, "Every last one of them. And they will do anything and say anything to get it."

Needless to say, the girls were stunned. One of the girls broke the silence. "What are we supposed to do?" she asked.

The girls were all looking at me as though they believed I had all the answers. I needed to breathe some hope back into this conversation and into the minds of these girls. I decided not to answer too quickly.

I was still formulating my response when Melissa blurted, "Get a vibrator."

Okay, that was not exactly what I wanted to say to a group of young and impressionable girls. But it was too late. We had a good laugh.

As an afterthought, Melissa said, "I've been with guys and afterward I thought, 'I could have done this myself and better.'"

This was followed by more laughter. It did not occur to me until later that night that none of the girls asked, "What's a vibrator?"

As we get older, the dating pool is either almost empty or very murky. It seems there is no one suitable to date. Most of the "available" men are throwaways, discarded by women who have had enough. For the most part, when you meet these men, they seem perfectly normal. So you have to wonder why they were discarded. What did they do? What didn't they do? Should I hire a private detective? Should I call the ex-wife or ex-girlfriend? These are perfectly legitimate questions. But, typically, it ends there. Instead, we take the plunge and go through with the date. Sometimes, we know during the first date that it was a big mistake. We may not even get through dinner. By the way, if he treated you to a TV dinner, don't bother with dessert.

Occasionally, you meet a great guy. He says all the right things. He is attentive and responsive. He compliments you. He dotes on you. He tells you he has never met anyone like you. He wants you to meet his friends, family, etc. He starts talking about the future and it includes you. Wow! This could be the one, but how can you be sure? The first thing you need to do is slow down. Do not rush into a relationship before you even know his full name and date of birth.

A few years ago, I went with three of my girlfriends, Brenda, Bea, and Emma, to have drinks at a hotel lounge. Sitting nearby was a group of about eight men who were also having drinks. About half an hour later, the server brought a drink to Emma, which was sent to her by one of the men. From our table, Emma tipped her drink at the man and took a sip. A few minutes later, she and Bea left the table and went to the bathroom. While they were in the bathroom, I was bored. I decided I'd have a little fun. So I took a book of matches that was on our table. I opened the flap and wrote, "Jack Meoff 969-1069." I closed the flap and waited.

When Emma and Bea returned to the table, I whispered to Emma, "He brought you something. He said to give it to you after he leaves."

Emma, of course, could not wait. She automatically assumed that the man who had sent her a drink had given me something to give to her. This was exactly what I wanted her to think. Anyway, I let Emma whine, and then beg, before I passed her the book of matches. I was careful not to let anyone see.

Emma opened the flap and whispered, "Jack Meoff, Jack Meoff, Jack Meoff." Then she asked, "Why does that sound so familiar?"

Bea just looked at me and shook her head. Emma was still looking at the name on the book of matches.

Then she said, "Emma Meoff. It sounds weird."

By then, Bea, Brenda, and I were trying very hard not to laugh. Finally, Bea turned to Emma and said, "Honey, read it again carefully. It says 'jack me off.'"

When Emma realized what it meant, all she asked was, "So he's not going to marry me?"

Take your time and evaluate everything about him. Your gauge is about five to six weeks. Keep track of the number of weeks you have been seeing each other. This should be easy since you usually keep track anyway. After you have been dating about five to six weeks, you get the first hint of trouble. This is about the time he lowers his guard, or drops it altogether. You might inadvertently find out some of his problems, or he may mention them. His true personality also emerges right about now. All of a sudden, the man you thought was perfect six weeks ago is disintegrating before your very eyes. Take the following into consideration.

<u>Financial Problems</u>: During the first few weeks of dating, money is usually no problem. A man will treat you to expensive dinners. He consistently finds time to take you to lunch. He promises to take you on wonderful vacations to exotic places. He buys you nice presents. He refuses to let you treat him. He does everything to give you the impression that he is a big man with a big bank account. One day, he mentions something about money or lack thereof. Here we go again, another one with money problems. He might be behind in paying his child support. Of course, he blames his ex-wife for being greedy during

the divorce. He might tell you that his ex-wife spends all of the child support on herself or on her new boyfriend. He might be having trouble paying his mortgage or paying his auto loan. He might still be making payments on a ring he bought his last girlfriend. She refuses to return the ring until he pays off the loan she co-signed for him two years ago. She co-signed the loan because he has bad credit, which he blames on his ex-wife as well. The fact that he has financial problems should raise a red flag. If you are earning any kind of decent money, he is counting on your weakness for him to help him. After all, if you love him, you have to help him. The chance that he will ask you for money is about seventy-five percent. The chance that he will pay you back is less than ten percent. You do the math.

A man with financial problems will plague the relationship. It is doomed. If you marry a man with financial problems, chances are you will get stuck with his debt, with the exception of his child support payments. However, do not be surprised if you end up having to pay for that, too. If you file a joint income tax return, and he has any liens filed against him, there is no refund. The Internal Revenue Service will seize the refund and send it to his ex-wife for her kids. And you thought you were going to pay off a few bills of your own or take a vacation. That is not going to happen, and you are going to be very pissed off.

<u>Personal Hygiene</u>: My friend Dolores once asked me, "Why do women rub their eyes in the morning?" When I couldn't answer, she said, "We don't have balls to scratch."

Yuck is right! You notice that every time he goes to the bathroom, he returns in less than one minute, sometimes in less than thirty seconds. What does this tell you? It tells you that he touched "it," and he did not wash his hands. So keep him away from that bowl of peanuts on your coffee table. For that matter, keep him away from all of your finger foods. If this happens at his house, do not eat anything. If you are hungry, you might want to steer him back to the bathroom and tell him to wash his hands. However, there is no easy way to tell him to wash his hands. You might need to develop a plan.

Plan A is the Indirect Approach. When he comes back from the bathroom, ask him, "Are your hands clean?" He'll look at them and his answer will be yes. Plan B is the Direct Approach. This requires that you are confident that he did not wash his hands—less than thirty seconds. Point to the bathroom and tell him, "Go back in there and wash your hands, you filthy, disgusting pig!" I do not like either plan. Plan C is the Direct But Non-Offensive/Passive-Aggressive Approach. At all times, carry waterless soap. All you have to do is squeeze some on his hands, tell him to rub his hands together, and forget about it. Keep in mind that this habit started at childhood. It could take years to correct. It could also be compounded by other disgusting habits.

You should also be concerned if he bites his fingernails in front of you and spits them out into the atmosphere. If you are at his house and he bites his toenails in front of you, tell him you will be right back. Then grab your purse, quietly pull out your car keys, tiptoe out the front door to your car, and drive away. Do not come back, and do not take his calls. It's over, baby. If he is at your house and he bites his toenails, tell him that you feel sick, and you should, and kindly ask him to leave. Then puke, if you must.

Remember, once a slob, always a slob. Unless you, too, live like a slob, you are not going to like this about him. If you are not a slob, you are going to find yourself cleaning up after him … constantly and forever. If you have already made the mistake of cleaning up after him at his house, believe me, he thinks you are a keeper. If his mother is still coming over to clean his house and do his laundry, he might have a syndrome. "Mama's Boy" should come to mind. This is not a good thing. This man will never find <u>any</u> woman who is as good as his mother. You cannot compete, so don't even try. He will always use his mother as ammunition against you because his mother is perfect and you are not. Let it go, and let him go, as well.

Now let's talk about belching and farting. While women find these two habits disgusting and annoying, men find them amusing. I suppose belching is not as disgusting as farting. However, it is disgusting when a man belches, and then he makes a joke about how it still smells like the

Chinese food he had for lunch. Women just do not find this funny in the least. By the way, if his mother catches him belching, she will poke him in the ribs or slap the back of his head, depending on how disgusted she feels. But you must remember, this is her little boy. Anything he does will always be so cute and precious, no matter how old he is and how revolting he acts.

There is no nice way to talk about farting. While this is a human bodily function, it is certainly not very ladylike. I do not know any women who fart around each other. We do not like to talk about farting. Think about it. The only time women use the word "fart" is when we use the word "men" in the same sentence. That is it.

On the other hand, men love to fart and love to smell their farts. Men also like their friends to smell their farts. They share their farts, and they try to combine their smells. Some men even bite at their farts. They have no problem farting in public, in the elevator, in their cars, in their offices, or in their bedrooms. It is simply gross and disgusting.

The only time farting in public is excusable is when it happens by accident. It just slips out. My friend Delia told me a story about a "captive fart."

She said, "I had been dating David for about two months. We saw each other nearly every day. We liked each other very much. We spent the day at the beach, and we were now heading back home. There was a long stretch of highway before coming to the next convenience store. I noticed that David suddenly became rather quiet. I asked him a couple of times if he was all right. He just nodded. I could not put my finger on it. He seemed uncomfortable or something. He mentioned that he wanted to stop and gas up at the next stop. I did not know that he already was ... gassed up. We saw the convenience store from a distance. He seemed to relax a little, but he was still quiet. We pulled up to one of the gas pumps. Instead of pumping the gas, he walked inside the convenience store with me. I missed a step and lost one of my sandals. I turned around to retrieve my sandal. David, who was following me, bent down to pick it up, releasing the captive fart. It was very loud, but rather short, like it had a shut-off valve. I could tell he had stopped it from releasing completely. I did not know if I should say or do anything. I knew I could not pretend I had not heard it. Poor David. He had the most agonizing look on his face. I could tell he was terribly embarrassed. He handed the sandal to me without looking at me.

"He quietly said, 'Sorry, babe.'

"I just took my sandal, put it back on, and continued into the store. He went straight to the bathroom. I did not know if he would ever have the courage to come out. I bought some chips, but I put the bubble gum back. I was afraid if I blew and popped a bubble, it would remind us of 'the incident.' The rest of the drive home was unbearable for both of us. I could tell he just wanted to get me home and never see me again. We continued dating for a while, but we both knew that the release of the captive fart was the defining moment in our relationship. Nothing was ever the same."

Delia continued, "So what did I do? I moved on. I met a man with a wonderful personality. Everybody loved Larry. He had a great sense of humor. He was charming and very engaging. I remember the first time he farted in front of me. It was right after he said, 'Pull my finger.' Like an idiot, I pulled his finger, and he let one fly. It was a loud and long whistling fart, followed by mini-farts. I let go of his finger the way you might let go of a hot iron. I think I called him a pig. He laughed so hard. He grabbed me and held me until I laughed with him. Then, I married him."

Everyone belches and farts. However, you have to decide if you want to be with a man who belches and farts in public. Once he feels comfortable enough to do this in front of you, he'll never go back to doing this privately. You have to decide if this is a habit you can learn to embrace.

<u>Past and/or Present Relationships</u>: At the beginning of the relationship, a man might tell you that he has only had three serious relationships with women. Later, you might find out that he was married to all of them. Initially, he might have passed himself off as a single man. However, you find out that he is actually working on his third divorce. He has children from all of his marriages. His total child support

payments almost exceed his monthly income. He somehow forgot to tell you that he sort of has a girlfriend, but he is going to break up with her. He can't break up with her just yet because she might be pregnant. Of course, he isn't sure if he is the father.

If he constantly talks about his last girlfriend or ex-wife and how much he loved her, he is not over her. Don't be surprised if he continues to call his ex-girlfriend and try to get back with her or just try to have sex with her. He may even try, for as long as he can (i.e., until he gets caught), to maintain two relationships, one with you and one with her. This is much more common than we realize. Most of us can name at least one ex-boyfriend who cheated on us while we were dating them. If he has a large number of ex-girlfriends, you may want to know the date of his last physical examination. Open his medicine cabinet and take note of any prescription medication he takes regularly. You're wondering, "Isn't that snooping?" Of course, it is. So what! Let's see, would you rather be called a snoop or would you rather be infected with a sexually transmitted disease? Snoop doesn't sound so bad, does it?

Sandy shared the following story and her "brush" with death.

She said, "When I was about fifteen years old, I liked this very cute guy named Danny. He had just turned seventeen. We met during the summer at the local swimming pool. We spent the summer swimming, diving, and eating snow cones. He was invited to a friend's birthday party, and he asked me if I wanted to come with him. I wanted to go to the party. I was going with my family on vacation the following day, so I would not get to see Danny again for two weeks. My mother agreed to let me go. It was a date, but my mother dropped me off at the party. She said she would be back at 11:00 p.m. I had hoped I could stay out until midnight. Danny was there when I got to the party. He looked even cuter in jeans and a T-shirt. We danced to very loud music, and we sat closely together in the dark, his arm around my shoulder. We kissed a few times, though it was a bit awkward. Later that night, we kissed again. This time, the kisses were wet and wonderful. I had never kissed like that before. It was the most romantic night I had ever spent with a guy.

"About an hour before my mother picked me up, Danny casually mentioned, 'Last week, I had to go to the doctor to get a penicillin shot.' My head started spinning. He continued, 'My uncle got me a girl in Mexico for my birthday. Now, it burns every time I pee.' I don't remember the rest of what he said. All I kept hearing was 'It burns every time I pee. It burns every time I pee. It burns every time I pee.' The words were getting louder and louder in my head. I had a horrible feeling in the pit of my stomach. I was going on vacation and I had syphilis or something, all from kissing. I felt nauseous. I asked Danny if he would go and get me something to drink. As soon as he left, I started spitting. I spit until I had nothing more to spit out. I then took someone's drink and used it to gargle and spit some more. A couple of people saw me, but nobody said anything. Danny came back with a drink and asked if everything was all right. I said everything was fine, but it was not. I excused myself and went to the bathroom. I locked the door and found a strong mouthwash in the medicine cabinet. I gargled until I gagged, and then I spit it out. I then took a capful of mouthwash and swallowed it slowly. I could not wait for my mother to pick me up. She arrived right on time. I had never been so happy to see her. I said some quick goodbyes and darted for her car. Days later, I was still terrified that it was going to burn when I urinated, but it never happened. My parents would have killed me. So much for the most romantic night of my life."

If you sign on to be in an exclusive relationship with a man, make sure the understanding is mutual. This usually happens after several months of dating. Sometimes, this happens even sooner. Both of you realize that you do not want to date other people. The problem is that some men—okay, most men—given the opportunity to have sex with another woman, will simply ignore the fact that he has a girlfriend. After all, this will only hurt you if you find out. He truly deludes himself into believing that he has to keep this from you for your own good.

My friend Kathy told me about how a wonderful relationship with Robert had suddenly ended. She and Robert had met while they were both working in the same building. They had now been dating for several months. Kathy was once divorced, with no children. Robert was once divorced, with two teenage children. Robert lived about forty miles from Kathy's house. Robert always found time after work to see Kathy before he went home. They saw each other mostly during the week. They had been talking about going to see the movie *Lethal Weapon 2*, and they had agreed to go together. One Tuesday, Robert drove his son to his ex-wife's home, which was 225 miles away. Robert returned alone the following day. Kathy saw Robert the rest of that week, but not on the weekend. The following Monday, Robert started making comments about the movie. Kathy started to suspect that he had gone to see the movie without her. When she asked him, Robert denied it. During the next few days, Robert said some things that made Kathy ask Robert again if he had gone to see the movie. Robert finally told her the "truth." He told Kathy that he had taken his son to see the movie. Robert told Kathy that he would take her, if she wanted to go.

The next day, Robert called Kathy and asked her if she wanted to go to lunch. Kathy agreed. She told Robert to meet her by her car in the parking garage. When he arrived, Kathy was waiting outside of her car. She was holding a calendar.

The first thing Kathy said to Robert was, "I can't prove who you took to see *Lethal Weapon 2*, but I can prove that you did not take your son."

Using the calendar, Kathy showed Robert that on Tuesday, he had taken his son to San Antonio. He had not returned until Wednesday. The movie, *Lethal Weapon 2*, had not opened until Friday, two days later.

Kathy then told Robert, "See, it is physically impossible for you to have taken your son to see this movie because your son is still in San Antonio."

Robert drew a long breath, exhaled, and then said, "You got me."

He never did tell Kathy who he had taken to see the movie. Kathy understood that he was seeing someone else. He lived forty miles away from her, and he was not accountable to anyone. He had found the time and the opportunity to date someone else. It was that easy.

Criminal History: Another thing you might find out around week six is that he is a criminal. After all, he cannot hide from his probation officer forever. Whatever he was convicted of, he will minimize it or just blame it on someone else. It is not unusual for men to have one or more previous convictions for driving under the influence of alcohol and/or drugs, driving without a license, driving while suspended, possession of a controlled substance, battery, domestic abuse, injury to a child, violation of a protection order, possession of a concealed weapon, check fraud, and domestic abuse. Oh, did I mention domestic abuse twice? Some men enjoy domestic abuse. Seriously, if you find that your new boyfriend is easily angered and prone to violence, tell a grown-up … a very big grown-up. Then dump him. Change your telephone number if you have to. Move to a different city if you have to. Just keep him away from you.

As I was saying, the majority of these convictions could have resulted in probation, or probation with the condition for up to one year in jail. Look for one or more certificates of completion for anger management classes, parenting skills classes, and thinking errors classes. Depending on the offense of conviction, these are just some of the required classes to successfully complete a term of probation. You will most likely find these certificates stacked on the kitchen counter, among the pile of unpaid bills, next to the empty pizza boxes.

More serious convictions like assault with a deadly weapon, sexual assault, rape, lewd and lascivious conduct, vehicular homicide, manslaughter, murder, robbery, burglary, and possession with intent to deliver a controlled substance almost always result in prison time. Ex-convicts are an entirely different breed of men. Remember, once a con, always a con. In prison, convicts take one of two paths. They either turn to God or they turn to a prison gang. Those who turn to God can recite scripture at the drop of the soap. These convicts pray together and minister to the others. It is the best way for a convict to do his time. Convicts who don't turn to God turn to a prison gang. If the convict becomes a member of that prison gang, he is a member for life. He continues to be a member even after his release back into our society.

While in prison, the gang members will defend him, but it comes at a price. The price is anything the gang members want. Homosexual sex in prison is common practice. In prison, a man who participates in homosexual sex is not necessarily homosexual, only the act itself is. So you know he has been to prison, he has had sex with other men, and now he wants to have sex with you. Lovely! By the way, you do not need to wait six weeks to find out his criminal history. This information is available on the Internet and/or is public record at the county, state, and federal courthouses.

Melanie sent a story to me about a man she referred to as "Felony Fred." She wrote, "Last summer, I met what I thought was a man who was too good to be true. I was right. I met this guy at the Basque Festival, and we just hit it off. During the evening, he said all the right things. Every time I said that I had done this or that, he had, too. Every time I said I had been somewhere, he said he had been there, too. Like a moron, I gave this guy my telephone number that night. Big mistake! Lucky for me, I have the ability to run criminal background checks on all the men I meet. I found out that Felony Fred had a long criminal history. I called his 'employer,' and they had never heard of him. I had mentioned to Felony Fred that I worked at the federal courthouse. Still, he had the nerve to call and ask me out. I was stunned. I politely blew him off, and I never went out with him. Here is the kicker. Two months later, one of my girlfriends set me up on a blind date. The blind date was none other than Felony Fred. He denied everything. I never saw him again. I found out later that he was serving time in the state penitentiary."

Pay attention to everything. This information is essential in any new relationship. Incidentally, men with convictions for sex crimes, especially those crimes involving children, carry a huge stigma when they are released back into society. No matter where they live, they have to register as sex offenders. Registration is lifelong.

"Recreational" Drug Use and Alcohol Abuse: You might also find out that he is still smoking marijuana like he was during the '70s. I would find it a little weird to hear a forty-year-old man laughing uncontrollably at absolutely nothing. I would get very annoyed if he could not stop laughing because he saw that I was not laughing, which he found to be even more hilarious. Still, there is nothing worse than a man who says, "I have the munchies." Unless he is under twenty-five, I would not want him saying the word "munchies" in any sentence. Other drugs like cocaine, heroin, and methamphetamines are not recreational drugs. If he is using drugs, you will find out, his boss will find out, and eventually, so will the police. At the very least, you place yourself at great risk of getting arrested and going to jail. At the very worst, you risk getting addicted to these drugs, selling drugs to finance your addiction, and going to prison. Hint #1: Drug users do not like to use alone. Hint #2: Long prison terms are handed out like candy every day, even to women, and to women with children.

Alcohol abuse is another huge problem in many relationships. Everyone has a tolerance level for alcohol. I drink one wine cooler or a glass of wine, and I am going to get a serious buzz. Drinking a couple of beers on the weekends or enjoying a couple of glasses of wine with dinner is perfectly acceptable. However, you might find out he drinks a couple of beers or more on a daily basis, or that he consumes bottles of wine by himself. He might have a serious problem if he and his friends are polishing off bottles of liquor every night. Drinking to excess is a serious problem. If his friends and/or family members are making comments about his drinking, he might be an alcoholic. Don't be afraid to ask them. For your own good, as well as for his, they will talk to you about it. However, don't be surprised if the information is followed by, "But you didn't hear it from me."

Sara knew, firsthand, what it was like to be involved with an alcoholic. She shared the following story. "Bobby always had an excuse to drink, and he always drank to intoxication. Bobby and I were in a weekly bowling league. The bowlers were Bobby's mostly male co-workers, their wives and girlfriends. Bobby got drunk every Wednesday night. I knew he was going to get drunk, so I always drove home. More often than not, Bobby started an argument on the drive home. One time, he was yelling at me and accusing me of flirting with his friends.

When I stopped at a red traffic light, Bobby suddenly opened the car door, jumped out, and ran away. I had no idea where he had gone. When the light turned green, I went through the intersection. I found a place to turn around and tried to find Bobby. He was gone. All I could do was drive home and wait. Eventually, he showed up. After Bobby bolted from the car several different times, I stopped going bowling on Wednesday nights.

"One Thursday morning, I tried calling Bobby at home. There was no answer. By mid-morning, I still had not heard from him. I knew something was wrong because he always called. I was unable to reach him at work. Right before noon, Bobby's mother called me from the hospital and told me that Bobby had been in an accident. I rushed to the hospital and found Bobby's parents waiting outside his room. I quickly greeted them before I walked in to see him. Bobby's right leg and right arm were broken. His eyes were swollen shut. His face was badly bruised. When Bobby heard my voice, he started to cry. His face contorted and tears ran out the corners of his eyes. He reached a hand to me. Once again, he promised he would stop drinking. He did … for a while.

"I left the room to talk to Bobby's parents. Bobby's mother told me that he had crashed his truck into a large tree. Of course, he was drunk. He was so drunk that he could not explain to paramedics how he came to be more than forty feet from the wreckage. The passenger side of the truck had sustained the most damage. When the police had notified Bobby's parents about the accident, they worried that I was with him. Luckily, I was at home.

"I knew that Bobby was a terrific guy when he was not drinking. Bobby knew that he had a drinking problem, and he promised to quit drinking. During the two years that Bobby and I dated, Bobby 'quit' drinking a number of times. Sometimes, he quit for a couple of weeks. Sometimes, he quit for a couple of months. But, he always found his way back to a bottle of beer. He always had an excuse to drink again.

"Bobby asked me to marry him on New Year's Eve. He promised that if I married him, he would never drink again. He said that his only

New Year's resolution was to stop drinking. I desperately wanted to believe him. Bobby and I got engaged and set a wedding date for June. I believe that Bobby did not drink during this entire time. Even at our wedding, Bobby opted not to drink any wine or champagne. This was something we had discussed, so I was very pleased when Bobby honored my wishes. What I did not understand until later was that Bobby was an alcoholic.

"About six months after we were married, Bobby told me that he was going to a bachelor party. Bobby promised that he was not going to drink. Knowing that I would worry, Bobby called me several times from the party. Each time, he said he would be home in about an hour. The last time Bobby called, he said he would be home at 11:30 p.m. There was not a lot of traffic on our street. Every time I heard a car, I thought it might be Bobby. He was not home at 11:30 p.m., or at 12:30 a.m., or at 1:30 a.m., or at 2:30 a.m. I went through a roller coaster of emotions. At first, I was worried. Then, I got mad. Then, I got even madder. Then, I started worrying again. Finally, I made a deal with God. I promised that if He just brought him home safely, I would be eternally grateful. I also promised not to fight with Bobby. I just wanted him to come home.

"I was asleep when Bobby finally came home around 4:00 a.m. He made a lot of noise as he made his way through the house. He came into the bedroom and flipped on the light. I woke up, but I was careful not to say anything. Bobby must have been expecting me to be angry because he quickly tried to place all of the blame on me and away from himself.

"Leaning heavily on the dresser, he looked at me and mumbled loudly, 'I'm sick of being married to you. I don't even love you. I never have.' I sat on the bed and felt the tears welling up and stinging my eyes. I leaned my head back, hoping the tears would go away. Instead, the tears ran out the sides of my face. I quickly wiped my tears and got off the bed. I picked up the telephone and dialed Bobby's parents' telephone number. Bobby's father answered the telephone. I apologized for calling so late. Then, I told Bobby's father that Bobby no longer wanted to be married to me. I asked him to pick up his son. I left the bedroom and retrieved two very large garbage bags from the pantry. I came back to the bedroom and proceeded to stuff one garbage bag with all of Bobby's personal belongings. I put everything together: shoes, boots, aftershave, golf clubs, photographs, suits, shirts, underwear, etc. After I filled one bag, I proceeded to fill the other garbage bag. Then, I took one bag and dragged it through the house to the front door. I opened the door and, in one motion, threw the unsealed bag onto the front lawn. Most of the items spilled out of the bag. I went back to the bedroom to get the second bag. I dragged it through the house and threw it out the front door, as well.

"Then I came back for the third bag … the Dirt Bag. Bobby was still in the bedroom, his back against the dresser. He appeared to be in a mild state of drunken shock. It all happened so fast that Bobby did not even have a chance to react. I grabbed him by the shirt at the neck. As I pulled him through the house, I screamed at him, 'You're sick of being married to me and you've never loved me? Then, get the hell out of my house!' I threw him so hard out the front door that his feet actually left the ground. He rolled several times on the lawn before he came to a complete stop. I closed the door and locked it.

"Moments later, I heard Bobby's father drive up to the house. As I opened the front door, I heard Bobby tell his father, 'Look, Dad, she threw me and my stuff out of the house.' Bobby's father looked at his son with disgust and told him, 'Shut up and get in the car.' Bobby's father apologized for his son and returned to his car. Bobby continued to pick up his belongings off the lawn and stuff them into the garbage bags. His father waited for him in his car. When Bobby was finished, he put the garbage bags in his father's car and they drove away.

"An hour later, the telephone rang. It was Bobby. He was hysterical (yes, some men can become hysterical). He said that he was so very sorry. He cried and cried, and he said that he loved me. He said he missed me, and he wanted to come home. He promised that everything was going to be okay. I coldly asked him, 'Where are you now?' Bobby said, 'In my old room.' I said, 'You better make yourself comfortable. You're going to be there for a while. You are not coming back here.'

"For several weeks, Bobby would not leave me alone. He called several times a day. He came over every night. He begged me to take him back. He assured me that he would never drink again. He promised to do anything to get back with me, including seeking treatment for his alcoholism. I just did not care. When Bobby said that he was sick of being married to me and that he did not love me, something inside of me snapped. I was done with Bobby. I was done with the marriage. Less than four months later, I was divorced. I also took my maiden name back. To this day, I know that Bobby has never gotten over his drinking problem."

<u>Work History</u>: Take a close look at his present employment and previous work history. Unless he has a great job, he is going to lie about his job and about his income. He'll say he is a lawyer when he is actually a legal assistant. Most likely, he will exaggerate how much he earns. All of this is done to impress women. However, the truth always comes out later.

It has been my experience that the job most men lie about is law enforcement. At some point, a man will say that he used to be a police officer. Actually, he was a security guard. If he was not a police officer, he might say that he once took a test to become a state trooper, an FBI agent, or some other type of law enforcement officer. When you ask what happened, the most likely response is, "I missed the test by one point." He makes it sound as though he only missed one question. He fails to explain that he needed to score an eighty-five, and he got sixteen questions wrong. He probably did not even meet the minimum qualifications. He may even have failed the drug test or the psychological test. Why do men lie about this? There's just something about having a gun and a badge that makes even the puniest man feel powerful and confident. I think that men understand that some women are attracted to men in uniforms and men in uniforms with guns and badges in police cars, who can drive as fast as they want, and run through red lights. It is as close as they can get to being Superman. We all know that every man wants to be Superman.

Let me tell you that Superman is not super anything, except super stupid. He does not have a terrific work history. What he tells you about his work history will never match his written resume, unless he lied on his resume, too. Ask to see his resume. If he lets you see it, he is hoping that you have forgotten the lies he told you. Problem is that women never forget. We have a keen way of remembering everything. One of my girlfriends dated a man who said he was making "six figures" working for an Internet company. It turned out he was selling items on an online auction. He did not have a full-time job, and he was not making "six figures." He was denied unemployment benefits. Consequently, he could not pay his child support. Needless to say, he asked my friend for a small loan, which he promised to pay back in two weeks. She had the good sense to talk to her girlfriends, who talked her out of it. After she told him she could not loan him the money, he accused her of not wanting the relationship as much as he did. He stopped calling, and soon, he was dating someone else. Loser!

Another problem is that many men just cannot hold down a job. They go from one job to another, each time earning less than at the previous job. They work for temporary periods spanning a few months. Then, they quit, they get laid-off, or they get fired. Typically, men lose their jobs because they show up late for work or they do not show up at all. It is not uncommon for a man to want a day off to go golfing or fishing during a workweek. But, his request for leave is denied. What does he do? He goes anyway. Some men expect to get high-paying jobs although they have no college degrees, no credentials, and no experience. They dream of being lawyers and doctors, but they have absolutely no ambition. Beware of this type of man: the dreamer. He has a lot of dreams, but he never achieves any of them. Find yourself a doer. This type of man usually has a long list of accomplishments. He travels. He has a career. He builds things. If his mother tells you that he has been like this since he was a little boy, find a good reason to keep him. He will not disappoint you.

<u>Temporary Living Conditions</u>: It is not unusual for a man to temporarily return to his parents' home following a divorce. Oftentimes, the wife gets the home in the divorce settlement. However, it is unusual if a man is thirty years old, and he still resides at home with mom and

dad. If you get to meet his mother, she will want you to know all of the things that she does for him. She is hoping that you will take care of him. If she is cooking his meals, doing his laundry, and picking up after him, you might as well adopt him because you are going to be raising a child. If you do not already have children, he becomes your only child. He will expect to be the center of your universe. If he has been "temporarily" living with his parents for an extended period of time, he might realize that he needs a change of scenery. You might find him "temporarily" living with you next. However, don't expect him to offer to help you pay the bills and the rent or to buy any groceries. You should expect more dirty dishes. You should also expect to do more laundry, more cleaning, and you lose the remote control. Get the picture?

Susan couldn't wait to tell me her story about her ex-boyfriend, Albert. Susan started, "When I met Albert, he was a body builder. He was six feet tall, 190 pounds, and so handsome. We had been dating for about two weeks before I found out he was still living at home with his grandmother. He was thirty-two years old. At first, I figured he lived with his grandmother because she needed someone to take care of her. She didn't. From the first time I went to Albert's house, it was clear that his grandmother catered to his every need. She served his meals, brought his drink to the table, and served him seconds, if he wanted. She did all of his laundry and ironed his clothes. She even made his protein shakes.

"Since his grandmother did not have a mortgage on her house, Albert paid no rent. The only bill he paid was the telephone bill. I found all this out as we continued to date. What was even more troubling was that Albert's grandmother was on social security. It was her only source of income. She was on a tight budget. Still, she preferred having Albert at home because he provided her a sense of security. One day, Albert told me that he wished we could live together and get married. However, he also told me that he was hoping to get his grandmother's house after she passed away. He bragged that his aunts and uncles were so proud of him for taking care of his grandmother. He figured that as long as he was in her house until she died, his relatives would be less inclined to ever get him out."

Susan continued, "When I decided to go away to college, Albert and I stopped dating. We remained friends. I didn't see Albert for the next three years. During a summer break, I called Albert. He still had the same telephone number. He told me that his grandmother had passed away. His relatives had allowed him to remain in his grandmother's house until he was able to afford to live elsewhere. Little did they know that he had no plans to live any place else."

<u>Sexual Fantasies</u>: Remember to check the number of weeks you have been dating. If you are already having sex with him, he will start sharing his sexual fantasies, usually during sex. Be comfortable with what you are willing to do. If you are not, say so and mean it. If you insist that he use a condom and he refuses, get dressed. Do not compromise on this issue. You do not know where "it" has been. Regarding his sexual fantasies, do not let him wear you down with his constant whining. Do not be surprised if he smugly says, "I broke up with my last girlfriend because she refused to …" Don't believe him. The more likely scenario was that she told him, "Those are not toys, you sick and disgusting pervert. Those are tools." Hint: Beware of power tools.

Lucy shared a story about a man with sexual fantasies. She said, "I met a very nice-looking guy at the beach, where I was living one summer. A few weeks later, he started spending weekends with me. We were making love one night, when suddenly he asked if I would like to try something different. I thought, 'We've tried just about … oh.' Instantly, I knew exactly what he was talking about. Without having to say no, I told him, 'That's an exit, not an entrance.' He quit asking, and then he quit coming to see me."

Whatever problems he has, this is your moment. This is your opportunity to walk or run away. It is as simple as saying, "I want to break up." "It's not you, it's me" also works. If you cannot bring yourself to break up with him, call your girlfriends. They will break up with him for you. They can go to him as a group. They can tell him that after evaluating the relationship, they have decided that you need to break up with him. If that does not work, have one of your friends ask him, "Have you ever heard the expression, 'She doesn't want to see your face, and she wishes you were dead'?" That should do it.

I wish I could say that as soon as the moment comes, most women do break up with Super Stupid. The reality is that most women do just the opposite. Do you know why? It is because women believe they can help men. Yes, that's right. Women develop the "Messiah Syndrome," believing they are saviors who were sent to save these men. A woman will believe that she, alone, can help him and save him. She believes that he will fall apart if she leaves him. She hopes that he will be grateful. In return, he will love her, and she will be worthy. And being worthy is a good thing, isn't it? Actually, I also think that women stay because they have already invested six weeks of their time. They remember how good it was at the beginning. That is the drug. That is the addiction. It was just great in the beginning when he was wonderful and everything he said and did was perfect. But now, it is all gone. He is gone. Maybe he never existed. Even as you look at him now, all that remains is the shell of a man that once was. NEXT!

3.

I Can Kill My Own Spiders

A woman called her husband and said, "Honey, I think there's something wrong with the car."
He asked her, "What's wrong with it?"
She said, "I don't know, but I think there is water in the carburetor."
The husband asked, "Where is the car now?"
The woman said, "Well, it's in the lake."

—Unknown

Did I mention I wanted to be Cinderella? I prefer the post "the glass slipper fits" and the post "she marries the handsome prince and lives in a beautiful castle" Cinderella. However, married or otherwise, most women are pre "she meets a handsome prince and they live happily ever after" Cinderella. The hard truth is that in our society, women do everything for themselves. We buy homes, negotiate car deals, manage bank accounts, plan vacations, schedule all kinds of appointments, wait for the cable guy, go to home improvement stores, move furniture, mow the lawn, and take the kids camping. Then the following day, we … The list is endless!

Women do have to fend for themselves. I know that I can do just about anything I put my mind to. I do not ever want to have to depend on anyone, especially a man, for anything. When I was going to college, I enrolled in a self-actualization class. One of the first assignments required that each student pick a descriptive word(s) that started with the first letter of the student's first name. Next, we had to add our name to the descriptive word(s). I picked Self-Sufficient Sylvia. At the time, I was single and living alone, and I did everything for myself. I owned my own home. I owned my own car. I had a good-paying job. I paid my bills on time. I maintained a savings account. I did not need anyone to take care of me. I still don't.

There is a huge difference between wanting a man in your life and needing a man in your life. I do not need a man, but I do want the man I have. Realizing that you do not need a man to take care of you can be very liberating and empowering. Even now, I can't think of one very good reason why a woman needs a man. Honestly, I could do without washing my truck and filling up the gas tank. However, I can do both, and I do both. And the sun still comes up every morning, and I continue to breathe in and out.

My friend Patty told me the following story. "I got married when I was still in high school. Eighteen years later, I had two daughters attending junior high school. I had a good job and a good marriage. I never saw it coming. Sam came home one afternoon. He wanted a divorce. He did not love me anymore, and he wanted a chance to start over. I was thirty-six years old, and I was alone for the first time in my life. I was consumed with grief. I was also terrified. Sam, who was very controlling, had always made the decisions. He picked out our house. He bought our vehicles and kept up the maintenance. He managed the finances. He was also a very picky eater. Over the years, my daughters and I learned to enjoy what Sam liked to eat. It was all about Sam. Now, he was gone.

"One day, while grocery shopping, I automatically reached for the brand of cookies he liked and put them in the shopping cart. I found myself staring into the cart at the package of cookies. I reached into the cart and grabbed the cookies. I wanted to stomp on the cookies and crush them into little bits. Instead, I put them back on the shelf and looked for the cookies I liked. For as long as I could remember, I had never bought the cookies I liked because I had talked myself into believing that I liked the cookies that Sam liked. I hated those cookies. I never ate one again."

Patty told me, "I knew I was going to be all right. I stopped renting 'action' videos and started renting videos about love and romance. I joined a yoga class. I made a point of having a girls' night out, something I had never done in eighteen years. I cut my hair. I even went on a singles' cruise to the Caribbean. I had always wanted to go with Sam on a cruise. Of course, he always had an excuse why we could not go. I knew I would never allow this to happen to me again. I realized that I liked the new me. It was a part of me that I did not even know existed. My friends, my family, and my daughters also liked the new me. It took me a long time to find out who I was, what I liked, and what was good for me."

Women forget just how special they are. The biggest problem is that men do not take any interest in us. They have no idea what we like and don't like. They don't ask us what we want. They don't care if we have dreams. They won't help us accomplish our goals. It does not help that we get so caught up in our careers and our families and their needs that we forget we are equally important. We spend so much of our time taking care of our homes, our husbands, and our children that we no longer find or have time for ourselves. I asked my husband once what he loved most about me. He said, "I love that you always take care of me and Lisa." I know that was a huge compliment. However, while I was busy taking care of them, there was no one taking care of me. I was too busy to take care of myself. I decided that I had to come first sometimes. I needed to stay both physically and mentally healthy. I found more time to ride my bike. I found more time to spend with my girlfriends. I found more time to spend alone. I enjoyed the fact that even when I was alone, I could entertain myself.

Stop and ask yourself, "Who am I? What do I want for me? What are my strengths?" If you think about it, you can list a number of things that define who you are. If you ask your girlfriends, they will list everything they love about you. They can list your skills. They can also list your accomplishments. I listed some of my skills and accomplishments. After I read them, I felt very proud of myself.

1. I can install a ceiling fan, and I can manage minor plumbing.
2. I am resourceful and good at finding great bargains.
3. I can hook up a surround sound system and program a VCR.
4. I can drive a motorcycle.
5. I make friends easily.
6. I have been to a Yankees game.
7. I am a great cook.
8. I am a good sister.
9. I gave birth to a baby girl, and I am a good mother.
10. I am a good wife.
11. I am trustworthy and loyal.
12. I can translate the Spanish language to the English language and the English language to the Spanish language.
13. I can read a map and follow directions.
14. I survived Basic Training.
15. I have thrown two live hand grenades, and I can shoot a handgun with precision.
16. I am empathic, and I always find goodness in everyone.
17. I am patriotic.
18. I donated a kidney to my father (I am going to Heaven).
19. I have lived in a foreign country without my parents.
20. I graduated from college with honors.
21. I am a very well-respected professional/career woman.
22. I can kill my own spiders. (I do not know what to do with them after I kill them. I'm still working on that.)

Now that you have read my list of skills and accomplishments, stop and make your own list. Be generous and do not be shy. If the list is too short, ask the people who love you to help you add to your list. You might be surprised at just how many skills and accomplishments you can add to your list. Find some time to share them with your girlfriends. Then, take the time to feel very proud of yourself.

4.
The Worst Thing About Motherhood...

A boy showed up for Bible study. The teacher asked him, "Bobby, I thought you were going fishing with your daddy. Did God help you choose to come to Bible study instead of going fishing?"

Bobby said, "No, he didn't. My dad said I had to come to Bible study because he didn't have enough bait for the two of us."

—*Unknown*

I was walking to work one morning when I overheard two women talking. One said to the other, "The worst thing about motherhood is trying to raise two teenagers at the same time."

The other woman responded, "I think the worst thing about motherhood is getting up in the middle of the night with a sick child."

All I could say to them as I passed them was, "No, the worst thing about motherhood is fatherhood."

They laughed, and agreed with me.

Most men believe that women are primarily responsible for the care of the children. If a man has to take care of his children for a couple of hours, he calls it "babysitting." The problem is that you do not babysit your own children.

I had not planned to have children. I had a dog. He was my baby. When I started dating my husband, all he talked about was having a baby. He was relentless. He would tell his friends that he was trading in his bow and arrows for diapers and formula. That was just so precious. About a week after we started dating, Ken gave me a beautiful pink baby dress. He also gave me a romantic greeting card. The postscript inside the card read, "The baby dress is for our daughter some day." There was no question that I would marry this man. At that moment, I closed my eyes and thanked my fairy godmother.

Things do not always work out this way. Christina shared her introduction to motherhood. Although her daughter was now seven years old, Christina became visibly upset as she told her story.

"One evening while I was still on maternity leave, I was running a slight fever. I had a terrible headache, and I knew I was coming down with something. I was still having pain from my C-section. I was curled up on the couch next to Michael, who was watching television. He knew that I was not feeling well. Somehow, he found it in his heart to say, 'You better go to bed now because you are not going to want to get up with the baby later.' There it was. Even being sick did not count. He was not planning to get up with the baby, not then, maybe not ever. I was in big trouble. Since the birth of our daughter, I had gotten up with her every night. It felt like an eternity. I knew Michael could hear the baby crying, but he pretended to be asleep. I was exhausted, I was sick, and I had to do this for the rest of my life. But all hope was not lost. I asked Michael to hand me the telephone. I dialed my parents' telephone number. When my mother answered, I told her that I was not feeling well, and I would not be able to get up with the baby for her late-night feedings. My mother paused for a second or two, and then said, 'We will be there in fifteen minutes.' I half expected her to ask me, 'Why can't that son of a bitch get up with the baby?' Whatever my mother was thinking, she kept it to herself and never mentioned it. Fifteen minutes later, my parents arrived.

"Michael did not say a word. I knew he was terribly embarrassed that my parents were coming to spend the night to help take care of the baby and me. Michael knew, or should have known, that it was his responsibility, as a parent, to take care of the baby. He also should have known that it was his duty, as a husband, to take care of me. You know, the old 'in sickness and in health' thing from our wedding vows. Anyway, that night my parents took care of the baby. They took care of me. They took care of everything. Life was good that night. After that night, Michael and I took turns getting up and feeding the baby. I was greatly relieved that I would not have to do this alone."

Women bear most of the responsibility for the care of the children. We feed them, bathe them, and watch them take their first steps. We take them to doctor and dental appointments. We register them for school. We buy their school clothes and school supplies. We help with homework and school projects. We go to baseball games and soccer games and spend countless hours at the pool. We take them to birthday parties. We find and screen good babysitters. We get up in the middle of the night when our children are sick. We lose time from work when our children are sick. We take them to theme parks and water parks, and we pack their suitcases for vacations. We tend to their cuts, scrapes, and bruises. We help plan their graduation and help them with college applications. We help them plan their weddings. We are also present at the birth of their babies. Ever notice that when people are on television, they always say, "Hi, Mom." No one ever says, "Hi, Dad."

Some men delineate "daddy" jobs and "mommy" jobs. Needless to say, the list of "mommy" jobs is one hundred times as long as the "daddy" jobs. When my daughter was about four years old, she handed her daddy a rubber band and asked him to make her a ponytail. He refused to take the rubber band and in a child-like voice, he said, "I'm not the mommy; I'm the daddy."

My daughter said, "No, Dad, you're what the French call, 'Les incompetent!'"

It was a line from the movie *Home Alone*, and the delivery was perfect. Of course, I got blamed for the slam. Still, I was so proud of my daughter.

I could always count on my husband to entertain our daughter. He took her to the movies. He took her swimming and to play tennis. They played video games together. They always had a great time. One day, I came home and found them playing a board game on the floor. My daughter, who was about five years old then, seemed frustrated, and I could see that my husband was way ahead. I waited for him to make eye contact with me.

I mouthed to him, "Let her win."

He mouthed back, "Why?"

Frustrated, I went over to him and whispered in his ear, "Because you are a grown-up and because this is Candyland."

I have always been overprotective with my daughter. For a very long time, I was terrified of my daughter riding in a vehicle with anyone, including her dad. I took full responsibility for taking her to daycare and later to school and picking her up. On weekends, she was always with me. I took her everywhere. It was not that I did not trust my husband. I did, honestly. I just did not like the idea of my daughter riding in a vehicle with anyone, other than me, of course. I would not even let her ride a school bus. During field trips, I took time off from work, picked her up at school, and took her to the field trip myself. Neurotic, me? Perhaps. Nevertheless, it was a part of my life that I could control, until one day.

When we were living in Idaho, my husband called me one morning. He said he needed to go to Washington. It was going to be an overnight trip, and he was taking Lisa with him. She was about six years old at the time. I did not want him to hear the panic in my voice. I calmly asked him what time they were leaving. He said he wanted to leave about 10:30 a.m. It was now 8:30 a.m. I had plenty of time to make a list of things that my daughter would need on the trip. I started working on the list:

blanket, pillow, change of clothes, extra pair of shoes, toys, crayons, coloring books, snacks, drinks, toothbrush, toothpaste, sunscreen, and towel. As I worked on the list, I answered a few telephone calls. At 9:45 a.m., I finished the list and called my husband at home. There was no answer. I figured that he was probably in the garage putting things in the truck. I called his cellular telephone, and he answered after the second ring.

I said, "Hey, it's me. I have a list of things that you need to pack for Lisa."

All I heard was, "Uhhhhh."

I said, "What do you mean 'uhhhhh'?"

He said, "Well, we're in Oregon."

Now I could feel the panic starting to set in. I could also feel a lump rising in my throat. I found it difficult to swallow. I did not want to get mad because there was absolutely nothing I could do. I took a deep breath, closed my eyes, and shook my head.

Calmly, I asked, "Did you take a pillow and a blanket?"

He asked, "What for?"

I did not bother to explain. I then asked him, "Did you pack her a change of clothes?"

He said, "She's not going to get dirty. She can wear the same clothes tomorrow."

My final question was, "Did you at least take her toothbrush?"

He said, "She can brush her teeth when we get back."

Then he said, "She'll be fine. Love you. We'll call you later. Say bye to your mother."

I faintly heard Lisa say, "Bye, Mom. I'll be okay. I have my bag. Don't worry."

Then, nothing. I did not even bother to look at the rest of my list. I simply took it in my hand and crumpled it up, making a fist. I was speechless. I wanted to cry.

When Lisa said she had her bag, I knew exactly what that meant. The bag was a large, blue and white Hawaiian canvas sack. I had recently packed it myself. It contained everything on my list, except the pillow. I breathed a huge sigh of relief. Then I returned to what my daughter said before she hung up. "Don't worry," she said. I reminded myself to ask my daughter later what she meant by that. After they returned from Washington, alive, I asked my daughter why she felt it necessary to tell me not to worry. She said that she knew that there was a big difference between moms and dads. She knew that I was always worried about her.

She said, "If it was up to me, I would make rules about how children should be raised."

I asked her, "What kind of rules?"

She named a few rules before I realized I should write them down. These are some of her rules:

1. Never leave the kid with the daddy.
2. Never let the daddy feed the kid. (Chicken broth is not soup. Add noodles or something.)
3. Never let the daddy take the kid for the haircut.
4. Never let the daddy pick the clothes for the kid.
5. Never let the daddy blame the kid for his mistakes.
6. Never let the daddy force the kid to do his chores.
7. Never let the daddy take sides against the kid.
8. Never let the daddy take the kid to the pool.
9. Never let the daddy help the kid with schoolwork.
10. If you buy the kid a toy (electronic device), you have to buy one for the daddy.

After I read the list that my daughter made, I was very afraid to die. I knew that I needed to stay alive at least until she was eighteen years old. It was not as though I was dying at the moment. I did not have any life-threatening illnesses or anything. I had just never been more assured that my daughter needed me. I went so far as to make my sister promise to help my husband raise my daughter, in case anything happened to me. I formulated a plan in the event I would die when my daughter was still young. Then, I had a long talk with my husband. I told him that my sister and her husband could raise our daughter. I told him that my parents would also help. I told him that they would make sure she finished high school and went to college. I laid out a very intricate plan, which outlined how my daughter would be taken care of.

When I was done with my speech, he sympathetically said to me, "You are out of your mind. I am going to raise her alone. I won't need anyone's help."

There was something about the way he said, "I am going to raise her alone," that made me question why he had said it like that. Now, I had fear and paranoia. Since I am still alive, I am learning to live with my fear and paranoia.

My daughter later told me, "Mom, you're writing a book about funny stuff. The list was meant to be funny. Don't worry about me, Mom. You know my dad is a good guy. I can handle him."

She's right. She can handle her dad. After all, he is her biological father. Even so, there are so many men who are very abusive towards their children. I'm not saying that men don't love their children. However, I believe that men are more abusive to those they love the most.

I knew that married women with children were less likely to admit that their husbands were abusive towards their children. Therefore, I asked mostly divorced women how their ex-husbands treated their children. Almost all of the divorced women admitted that their ex-husbands had been abusive towards their children. I found these responses very sad.

1. He treated other people's children better than he treated his own.
2. He called our son a "fag" if he cried.
3. He ignored the children, and he only spoke to them to punish them.
4. He never once took them to a park or a movie.
5. He never took the time to help the children with homework.
6. He used to strike my son without provocation.
7. He deliberately played favorites with the children.
8. He cursed at the children and told them they were worthless.
9. He made my six-year-old daughter go to bed without dinner because she was "getting fat."
10. He never found time to go to my son's baseball games.

While many men are abusive toward their own children, they can be even more abusive toward their stepchildren. Those of you with blended families know exactly what I am talking about. Sometimes, men are just mean to children. If you have to question whether you need to contact the police and file a report, you should remove both your child and yourself from the relationship. If your husband, boyfriend, pig, Satan, whatever, does not like his children or your children, move on. Do this for the sake and safety of your children.

No one can protect our children better than we, as mothers, can. Put your children first. Make them your priority. They will remember you did this for them. My daughter and I have a standing joke.

She'll ask, "Mom, who do you love more, me or Grandpa?"

I'll answer, "That's a tough question. Ask me another one."

She'll ask, "Mom, who do you love more, me or Daddy?"

I'll answer, "That's easy. You."

I need my daughter to know that while I love her daddy, she is my priority. No one could ever love her more. Make sure your children know that.

5.

I Am, Therefore I Shop

One day, a woman decided that she would go out and buy a DVD player. Her husband had insisted that she buy another VCR. They argued about this issue for weeks. The woman reasoned that DVD players were "in" and "cool," and VCRs were "so yesterday." The man said that DVD players were no big deal, and he insisted that they purchase another VCR. Well, the woman did not want or need another VCR. It was time to buy a DVD player.

As the woman was leaving the house, her husband asked her, "Where are you going?"

The woman placed her hands on her hips, and with total defiance, she firmly stated, "Today, I will buy a DVD player."

The husband half jokingly and half sarcastically stated, "Let me remind you that I wear the pants in this family."

To which the woman responded, "Yes, but I'm the one with the balls in this family."

—Unknown

My husband does not like to shop. It is rare for us to go shopping together. We used to go shopping together, but he always managed to get lost. I used to spend half my time looking for him. Most of the time, he had gone back to the truck, where he was waiting for me. The only way I found out he was in the truck was because I had already looked every place else.

I could not exactly go to the customer service desk and say, "I lost my husband in the store. He is wearing a dark blue T-shirt, blue jeans, and sneakers. I last saw him in the sporting goods section." A woman's voice would sound over the loudspeaker and say his name for all to hear. Then she would say, "Your mother, I mean, your wife is waiting for you at the front of the store." And it would then be repeated. No way! Instead, I shop alone.

My good friend Dee is married to a man named Greg. Greg also does not like to shop. However, this does not prevent him from spending money ... a lot of money. He takes great pride in the fact that he owns so many toys, which fill his three-car garage. The first time I went to their house, I noticed two snowmobiles and trailer, a large raft, a fishing boat, several bicycles, and a motorcycle in the garage.

What bothers Dee most about Greg is that he spends nearly all of the money he earns on himself. Dee complained, "It took me a long time to realize that Greg was contributing very little of his income to our household expenses. At the beginning of the year, he traded his pick-up truck for a $55,000 Hummer. Greg said it was the perfect time to purchase a new vehicle. Even with a $3,000 down payment, his payments were almost $900 a month for seventy-two months. He was also spending about $200 a month in gasoline. He continued his health club membership, which cost $130 a month. In early May, he arranged to go on a hunting trip. The price of the hunting trip was $4,200. This did not include airfare, which cost $475. In June, he ordered a $2,200 laptop computer. He charged it. He was also paying $80 per month for cellular telephone service. In September, he went on the hunting trip. He took $1,200 in spending money. For his birthday in October, he purchased a big-screen television. It was on sale for $2,400. The extended warranty was extra. For Christmas, he decided he wanted a bicycle. We went to the bicycle shop together. I was shocked at the price. It was $1,700. He also purchased some accessories at a cost of $215. For Christmas, Greg also spent about $500 on Christmas gifts for the children and me."

When she mentioned this, we looked at each other and shook our heads. Then, we couldn't help but laugh. After all of the money he had spent on himself, all he spent on Dee and the two kids was $500. It took us a while to add up all of Greg's expenses. Dee didn't calculate Greg's other expenses, including weekly lunches and dinners that Greg treated his friends to and clothes that he bought for himself throughout the year. Even so, we calculated that Greg had spent more than $31,000 on himself. His yearly salary was just over $40,000.

Although Dee was upset with Greg, she was even more upset that she rarely bought any of the things she wanted to buy for herself. She didn't have any "toys." She spent money out of necessity. She bought things for the house, clothes for the kids, and always paid her bills on time. Dee took the list that we made, folded it in half, and put it in her purse. She was in a rush to leave. I knew how much this had upset her. I also knew she was about to put an end to this. All I could tell her was that she needed to put herself first sometimes. She needed to know that it was okay to treat herself to anything she wanted. She drove away.

I'm not advocating that women buy beyond their means. Spending money, within reason, is fine. One of the things that my husband finds irritating about me is my love for garage sales and my love for expensive things. This makes no sense to him. It makes perfect sense to me, so it does not matter if it makes no sense to him. At garage sales, I find used books, candles, candleholders, kids' toys, picture frames, crystal vases, and CDs, and I still have change from my $20. One Saturday morning, I went to some garage sales and bought a few things. I then went to the mall and found a great pair of designer shoes. I brought all my stuff inside and placed it on the counter. My husband looked over my things, and then he picked up the shoebox.

He noticed the price tag and asked me, "Why did you buy all this junk and then pay $165 for a pair of shoes?"

I responded, "Because I'm a princess."

See, when you don't have a good explanation, always revert to the fact that you are a princess. It is very hard to argue with that.

Anyway, when we moved to Idaho from Alaska, we signed a six-month lease on an apartment. I figured that this would give me plenty of time to find a realtor and find a house.

My husband said, "You are not going to find a house in six months."

What did he know? I was on a mission. My realtor put me on a homebuyer's program. This allowed me to view, online, all of the latest listings, based on my criteria for the home I wanted. Some of the listings included photographs and some included virtual tours. From my home computer, I was able to look at several hundred listings, some of which I liked.

I was always telling my husband, "Come look at this one."

He would wander over and take a look.

After a while, he only said, "Hon, just pick a house."

On several occasions, I went with my realtor to see several homes, but I did not like any of them. Five months later, I was still searching for a house. I went from leisurely looking for a house to frantically looking for a house. I was not about to let my husband's prediction come true.

One evening, I was on the Internet looking for home listings. I found a new listing for a townhouse, and it looked perfect. It was a stand-alone townhouse on a corner lot. The landscaping was beautiful, and I just had to see the inside. I dragged my husband over to the monitor so he could look at it. He seemed to like it, too. The next day, I called my realtor and told him about the listing for the townhouse. We agreed to meet later that day. Just as I thought, the townhouse was perfect. We made an offer, and after a few minor adjustments, the offer was accepted.

After signing all of the paperwork, we were ready to move. I had three days left on my apartment lease. I had made it. I took the afternoon off from work. With the help of my cousin and my nephew, my husband

and I packed our larger pieces of furniture and numerous boxes into the moving truck that my realtor let us use. When it was full, we drove to our new home with our first load. I opened the garage door and started unloading some boxes, which we each carried into the townhouse. As we walked inside, my husband looked around and then turned back to look at me.

He exclaimed, "Hon, this is so nice!" Even as he went upstairs, I could hear him say, "Wow, look at this place!"

My cousin turned to me with a puzzled look on his face. I explained, "This is the first time he has actually seen the house."

My cousin whispered, "You're kidding, right?"

He could not believe that my husband would let me buy a house he had never seen. This came as no surprise to me. I also knew that asking my husband to go shopping for window treatments was out of the question.

In November 2002, I went to Texas because my father needed a kidney transplant. I was the donor. The day before my kidney was removed, my mother and I went to the North Star Mall in San Antonio, Texas. I found some beautiful clothes that I just had to have. I blew over $1,100 in about three hours (lunch not included). The clothes I bought were timeless pieces. My mother said I deserved to buy myself whatever I wanted. And being the good daughter that I am, I did not want to argue with my mother. After all, I was having elective surgery in less than twenty-four hours. I did make my mother keep all of the receipts in case she needed to return everything.

When I returned home to Idaho, I made the mistake of leaving the price tags on the clothes. I should have removed them, but I was too busy doing laundry and cleaning up after being gone for sixteen days. I forgot. I went upstairs and found my husband in my closet. He noticed the charcoal-colored suit that was hanging on the clothes rack. He pushed aside some of the other clothes and reached for the sleeve of the jacket. I winced. He found the price tag and remarked, "You paid $325 for this suit."

I clarified, "No, I paid $325 for the jacket."

He raised his eyebrows, but he did not say anything else. He walked out of my closet without looking at the rest of the price tags. Whew! He had no business in there to begin with. I must say that he loved the suit, and he never again mentioned the price.

Do you want to know what is wrong with buying nice things? Absolutely nothing! Let's go shopping.

6.
When Intelligent Men Say Stupid Things

A man walked over to a woman and said, "Let's pretend we're carpenters. First, we'll go get hammered, and then I'll nail you."

The woman said to the man, as she looked down at his crotch, "You didn't bring enough wood."

—*Unknown*

Historically, there have been some very bright, intelligent, and powerful men—presidents, judges, congressmen, rising politicians, actors, and professional athletes—who have said or done some very stupid things to or with women. I'll bet at least one comes to mind. At this level of prominence, celebrity, and recognition, the old adage "Boys will be boys," is replaced with the new adage, "Men are so stupid."

You know the type: big egos, small penises. Always trying to overcompensate for their … uh, shortcomings. The men you are about to meet were my bosses, co-workers, and acquaintances. For the most part, these were men I worked closely with and initially admired. I pondered over how to tell these stories. Should I list them in alphabetical order, chronological order, or by the level of their stupidity? In the end, I opted to put them in chronological order. Of course, the names of these men have been changed to protect the innocent—their wives, children, parents, siblings, and friends.

Meet Jim: an extremely bright attorney, who had aspired to be a politician.

Jim was a very handsome man, even in his late fifties. He was married to a beautiful woman.

I worked for Jim in his law office. One day, we found ourselves working on a case that needed to be filed in court that day. We worked into the early evening and then sent a runner to the local courthouse, where a clerk was waiting for the filing. It was the first breather we'd had in hours, and we found ourselves alone in his office. Jim started talking about the day he hired me. He told me how very impressed he was with my level of intelligence. He also mentioned that he had hired me because he found me very attractive. Then, he dropped a bombshell!

He said, "I want to have an affair with you."

I stared at him blankly, not knowing quite how to respond. "He did say affair," I thought to myself. Finally, I asked, "You want to have an affair with me? Like right this minute?"

He just looked at me. He had not anticipated my reaction. Maybe he thought I would find his offer so terribly irresistible that I would tear off my clothes and have sex with him on top of his desk. Keep dreaming!

I looked at him and sarcastically remarked, "I never thought I would ever hear someone say, 'Hey, Sylvia, you want to have an affair?' And I would snap my fingers and say, 'Sure, Jim, when can we start?'" Then I just stared at him.

He pointed to the door and said, "Get out."

Yes, I continued working for Jim. He never hit on me again. However, he found new ways of being mean. He was also very rude, especially in front of my co-workers or clients. One day, I must have been particularly sensitive or maybe he was just mean. I don't remember.

What I remember is that I was upset with Jim. It was closing time. I was preparing a bank deposit in the reception area. The other employees had gone home. Jim was in the same reception area, lying down on a couch that was next to the front door. He was waiting for some clients. He was trying to make small talk, but I just answered him with a "yes" or a "no." Still in his prone position, he asked what was wrong.

I said, "Nothing is wrong. I just want you to know that today is your lucky day."

That immediately piqued his interest. He sat up and asked, "What do you mean it's my lucky day?"

I placed the deposit in the bank bag, grabbed my purse, and proceeded to the front door. I stopped and looked at him for a few seconds. Then I said, "If I went home and told my father how mean you are and how badly you treat me, he'd march into your office, drag you out of it, and beat the shit out of you. But I'm not going to tell him. That's why it's your lucky day."

Without giving Jim a chance to respond, I walked out the door. I continued working for Jim for another five months, but he was never mean or rude to me again.

About a year later, I ran into Jim in the cafeteria of the federal courthouse. He was having a late lunch. Foolishly, I walked over to his table to say hello. He greeted me warmly and asked how I was. He mentioned that he was trying to lose some weight and asked me how I managed to keep my weight down.

I told him, "I don't follow a diet. Sometimes, I just want to eat two scoops of vanilla ice cream for breakfast. I do not eat eggs, bacon, toast, and the two scoops of vanilla ice cream."

He asked, "So what did you eat for lunch?"

I answered, "I had a bowl of peach cobbler."

Jim then asked, "What will you eat for dinner?"

I answered, "I don't know. It depends on how hungry I am."

He smiled before he asked, "Why don't you have me for dinner tonight?"

I answered, "Because I could never be that hungry." I thought, "Unbelievable!" It was time to go.

Meet Dave: an idiot, nerd, probably married the first girl he had sex with.

When I was working for the federal government, I worked in a male-dominated field. I was but one of a few female federal officers. Dave, one of my co-workers, was just plain stupid. He was always saying stupid things. If I seemed upset about something, he would say things like, "Looks like Sylvia didn't get any last night" or "She must be on the rag." Of course, it was always behind my back. One day, as I was leaving the judge's chambers, I saw Dave talking with a couple of FBI agents. I was wearing a cream-colored suit. The skirt fell just above my knees.

As I started walking towards Dave and the two agents, Dave said, "Hey, Syl, nice suit." But before I even had a chance to thank him, he added, "But don't you think your skirt is a little too short for court?"

I walked up to him, looked down at my skirt, and said, "Maybe it is too short for court. But your wife is a slob, and she is dog-ugly. You see, Dave, tomorrow I can get rid of this skirt, and it won't matter. But tomorrow, your wife will still be a slob, and she will still be dog-ugly."

I walked away, and I could still hear the laughter of the FBI agents as I boarded the elevator. I went back to my office and sat behind my desk. A few minutes later, Dave came in and closed the door behind him. I could see that his chin was trembling, and he wanted to cry. He was so angry about what I had said about his wife. He told me that I didn't even know his wife. He swore that she was not a slob, and she was not ugly. He also said he was just playing. He got through it without crying.

Then I said, "First, you started it. If you are going to play, you need to know that I never play fair. So, if you tell me that my skirt is too short, I am going to tell you that your wife is a slob and that she is ugly. If you criticize my hair, I am going to call your mother a whore. If you can't take it, don't play with me anymore." He didn't.

Meet Bob: Deputy U.S. Marshal, married with children.

One day, I found myself waiting for an elevator in the federal building. I saw Bob coming around the corner with several shackled prisoners. He greeted the court security officers with a simple, "Hello, gentlemen." As I moved back to let him and the prisoners pass by, Bob greeted me with, "How's it going, Legs." Never at a loss for words, this time I was stunned and embarrassed. Oblivious, Bob continued walking with his prisoners. I was fuming by the time I got back to my office. I just could not understand how he could be so blatant. "Legs." I played back the scenario, upset that I had not said anything at all. Later that day, I ran into Bob again.

I walked over to where he was and quietly said to him, "Bob, can you do me a favor?"

He said, "Anything for you, Legs."

I whispered, "In the future, please don't call me anything you can't call me in front of your wife, okay."

He didn't say a word. It was as if he was holding his breath. It was over. It never happened again.

Meet Mike: attorney, bright, intelligent, handsome, shameless flirt, and very married.

Every time I ran into Mike at the federal courthouse, I felt like I was being undressed. He was very good at it. He would start a conversation and make eye contact. Then he would look at me from head to toe, slowly and deliberately. It was the way you might look at dessert, and you just don't know where to take the first bite. He made me feel very uncomfortable. He was always asking me to have dinner with him, but I consistently turned him down. It got real old, real fast. He just did not seem to get the message. One day, he came to my office to ask about a client. Once again, he asked me to join him for dinner. I thanked him, but declined.

He said, "How about lunch?"

I took a deep breath. I told him that I appreciated how nice he was to me all the time. Then I proceeded to tell him that the reason I could not go to lunch, dinner, or anywhere else with him was because I had a serious medical condition. He looked very concerned and asked what was wrong with me. I told him I was too embarrassed to tell him. Still, he pressed. I relented, but not before making him promise not to tell anyone. He actually took his index finger, crossed his heart, and waited.

Finally, I said, "I'm allergic to married men."

He looked at me, confused, and then asked, "What does that mean?"

I said, "They make me sick."

He could not stop laughing. He finally said, "You got me. I'll leave you alone."

I had finally made my point, and he never again asked me out.

Meet Jonathan: attorney, big flirt, big man, over six feet tall, and old enough to be my father.

An FBI agent named Fred had arrested a fugitive who was to appear before our federal magistrate. Fred and I were waiting in the judge's clerk's office. We were standing on opposite sides of a doorway. Jonathan and his legal assistant entered the judge's office and asked if the judge was in. The clerk told him the judge was still at lunch. Jonathan said he would wait. As he turned around, he saw me. The look he gave me was lecherous. He never took his eyes off me. He walked right up to me and stood less than twelve inches away. He never even looked at Fred, who stood about two feet next to me. Jonathan, who towered over me, looked down at me and I met his eyes.

He said, "Darling, you don't know what you do to my ... heart."

Without losing eye contact with Jonathan, I pointed to the FBI agent standing next to me and said, "Jonathan, this is my husband, Fred."

Jonathan was aghast! I noticed that his legal assistant covered his face with his hands and dropped his head to his chest.

Jonathan turned to Fred and said, "I'm sorry, sir. I didn't mean to insult anyone."

Fred played along and said, "I think you owe my wife an apology."

To which Jonathan responded by bowing gallantly to me and saying, "Please forgive me."

Jonathan then quickly went to the door and motioned to his legal assistant to join him. They left.

Weeks later, I ran into Jonathan's associate. He walked over and said, "I heard what happened with Jonathan. I think that from now on, he's going to be admiring you from afar."

Meet Steve: co-worker, postal, needs to double his medication.

Steve was going through a tough time. His wife had left him for one of her former high school students. During his divorce, Steve had discovered that his wife had numerous affairs throughout their nine-year marriage. Still, he wanted her back. He came to my office one morning and asked if we could talk. I invited him to sit down. He told me how much he loved his wife. He believed they had a good marriage. He worried about how the divorce would affect his two children. For over an hour, I listened attentively. He cried and, at times, seemed inconsolable. It was very difficult to see him this way. When he had composed himself, we both stood up. I walked over to him and gave him a hug. I reassured him that everything would work out. He no longer seemed upset. Instead, he took a step back.

He had a stupid grin on his face, and then he looked down at his crotch and said, "Look what you did to me."

I looked down to find a little bulge and the faint appearance of a wet spot on his pants. Pointing to his crotch, I remarked, "It's tiny and it's crying. That's why your wife left you. Get out of here."

Meet Louis: attorney, a bit of an eccentric, brilliant, and annoying.

Louis and I were working on a research study that involved his expertise. I asked a lot of questions. However, he was usually too busy to help me or he would answer my questions with a question. It was very frustrating. Even if he was not busy, he looked annoyed that I would interrupt whatever important task he was doing, like reading the newspaper or checking his email. Louis did not seem to care that he was not well liked by the others in the office. At one time or another, he'd had a falling out with everyone, except me. Although everyone tolerated him, I was the only one who was nice to him.

One day I went to his office to ask him a question. Before I even had a chance to say anything, he put his hand out and said, "I can't help you. I'm not a people person today. Get out."

I stood there momentarily. Then, I turned and left. I did not see him the rest of the day. I did not want to see him the rest of the day.

The following day, I saw him walking down the long hallway towards his office. I looked up at him and told him, "Louis, you better be nice to me today. I already had to defend you once this morning."

He said, "Oh really, how did you defend me?"

I said, "Well, they were talking about you this morning."

Knowing that I was not going to tell him who "they" were, he asked, "Well, what did they say?"

I said, "They said you're obnoxious. But I defended you. I told them, 'He's not obnoxious; he's very obnoxious!'"

We both laughed, and he gave me a high-five.

Meet Frank: supervisor, loved to make jokes at the expense of others.

I was always on guard with Frank. I had heard him tell people things like, "That's a nice suit. Did they have any in your size?" I had also heard him tell people, "You know, you almost match today."

One day, he was in our office talking to some of my co-workers. As I passed by on the way to my office, he stopped his conversation. He looked me over and said, "Turn around."

I said, "Make me."

He said, "I'm serious. That suit looks tight on you. You better not go to court like that."

I could not imagine how the suit could look tight, since I am my own worst critic. I am very petite and I liked the fit. I had also gotten a number of compliments. I told him, "It might be snug, but it isn't tight."

Anyway, he finally made me turn around, all the while trying to convince my co-workers to go along with him. I noticed that he was wearing a pair of polyester knit pants. I told him, "Now you turn around."

As he made a complete turn, I pointed at his pants and said, "My suit might be tight, but you have panty lines."

Everybody started laughing, except Frank. He did not speak to me for about four months.

You might be wondering if I ever complained or reported any of these incidents as sexual harassment. I didn't because I didn't have to. First, I did not feel that I was a victim of sexual harassment. Once I confronted these men, the harassment stopped. That was my own experience. However, I strongly encourage a woman to file a report or complaint if she believes she is a victim of sexual or other forms of harassment in the workplace. Find out if your employer has a written sexual harassment policy. Then follow the grievance procedure. Good luck.

7.

A Woman Scorned

At midnight, a couple left a party. Just outside the city limits, they were pulled over by a state trooper. The trooper approached the couple's car. The driver handed the trooper his driver's license.

The trooper asked, "Have you been drinking, sir?"

The man replied, "I had a few beers at a party."

By the address on the driver's license, the trooper knew the couple was still quite a ways from home. The trooper was still shining his flashlight at the couple when he asked, "Does your wife drive?"

The man looked to his right and then back at the trooper and he said, "Yeah, she drives, but ... she's at home."

—*Unknown*

My first exposure to infidelity was when I was about fourteen years old. My friend, Sally, who was fifteen years old, had been babysitting for Eric and his wife, Maliya, for about two years. The couple had two young children. Eric, age thirty, was a handsome businessman, a rising politician, and he was having sex with a teenager. I don't know if Sally or

I even realized that it was against the law. After all, Sally, who was in love with Eric, was only afraid that her mother and/or Eric's wife would find out. Eric had promised Sally that he would divorce his wife when Sally turned eighteen. But Sally was still a teenager and Eric was married and thirty years old. The relationship was morally and legally wrong. It was like thirty going on thirteen, and thirteen going down on thirty.

Eric's wife did find out, and she was devastated. I imagine that Maliya started getting suspicious when Eric took longer and longer to take Sally home. One night, she put her children in her car and followed Eric, who had taken Sally home after a night of babysitting. Maliya saw Eric's car parked a few blocks from Sally's house. By the time that Eric and Sally realized it, Maliya was on the driver's side of Eric's car, pounding on the window. Although it was dark, she saw what Eric and Sally were doing. She was screaming at Eric and at Sally, and she was trying to open the car door. People in the neighborhood started turning their porch lights on. Eric managed to get out of the car to try to calm her down, to no avail. Maliya was slapping Eric and trying to get to Sally, who was still inside Eric's car. Sally managed to find all of her clothes. She opened the passenger side door and ran the rest of the way home.

Sally did not hear from Eric the next day or the day after that. Sally knew it was over when Eric's wife came to her house and told Sally's mother about Sally's sexual relationship with Eric. She waited with Sally's mother until Sally came home from school. Even though she was angry that Sally would allow this to happen, Maliya placed all of the blame on Eric. If Sally's mother thought about filing charges against Eric, she never brought it up. Clearly, this was a chargeable offense. She may have been worried that since the sex was consensual, it would only serve to embarrass her and her family. Unbelievably, Eric contacted Sally about two weeks later. He wanted to meet with her. He told her that he loved her and that he missed her. Fortunately, Sally's father had picked up another extension. He yelled at Sally to hang up the telephone. Sally could hear her father yelling, "She's fifteen! Did you hear me? She's fifteen!"

Incidentally, Eric achieved his political ambitions. He even served as a county court judge. Eric and his wife did not divorce until years later.

Eric's affair with Sally must have been one of the factors that eventually led to the dissolution of their marriage. The trust had been broken forever. The damage to the marriage was irreparable. Eric eventually remarried and had two more children with his new wife. My guess is that he and his new wife hired babysitters. I wonder how old they were.

This type of betrayal is compounded when a man has an affair with his wife's best friend. One afternoon, I was having drinks with my friends Gina and Eva. Gina's husband, Nick, had just started serving a three-year prison term following a felony drug conviction. Gina's twenty-year-old housekeeper, Mari, had mentioned to Gina that Nick had repeatedly made sexual advances toward her during the time that she worked in their home. Until now, Mari had been afraid to tell Gina. Although there had been no sex involved, Mari confided that Nick had repeatedly tried to kiss her. She also mentioned that Nick had often touched her inappropriately.

When Nick called Gina from prison, she confronted him about Mari's accusations. Gina warned Nick, "Don't lie to me. Tell me the truth. If you lie to me, it's over. I will not take the kids to see you, I will not take your calls, and I will not send you any money." Gina also told Nick that it did not matter what he had done in the past, that she would forgive him. She lied, of course. She just wanted to know the truth. Nick made Gina promise not to leave him. She crossed her fingers and promised.

With that, Nick conceded to Mari's accusations. Still, he made it seem as though he believed it had been consensual. Remarkably, he also admitted to a brief affair with Kathy, Gina's best friend. That revelation was completely unexpected. Gina and Kathy had been close friends since grade school. Several years back, Gina had hired Kathy to help her and Nick manage their small business. During that time, Kathy had lived with Gina, Nick, and their children, and had spent the holidays with them. On New Year's Eve, Gina recalled that she went upstairs to check on the children, and she found that one of them was still awake. Gina remembered that she put her head on the pillow next to her child and fell asleep. She did not wake until the following day. Gina did not know until years later that Nick had checked on her and found that she was asleep. Nick told Gina that one thing led to another, and he took Kathy out to the garage. There, they had their first sexual encounter. Nick told Gina that the affair had ended a few months later, when Kathy found out she was pregnant.

Gina recalled that Nick had told her that Kathy was pregnant. At the time, Gina had not questioned why Kathy had chosen to tell Nick about her pregnancy before telling her. Gina talked to Kathy, who wanted to have an abortion. Gina made the arrangements for the abortion and paid for the procedure. Gina even took Kathy to have the abortion. After the procedure, Kathy recuperated at Gina's house. Gina never suspected that Nick was the father of the baby Kathy aborted. What a pig!

After Gina finished her story, we all sat quietly, absorbing what we had just heard. We called the waiter over and ordered more drinks. If ever there was an I-really-need-a-drink kind of story, this was it. We were flabbergasted! I asked Gina if she had talked to Kathy. She had not, but she was planning to confront her.

Holding back tears, Gina said, "I am so angry! I could kill Nick for doing this! I don't want to see Kathy right now because I want to kill her, too! I wish I could kill them both!"

I said to Gina, "You know, that's not very nice. But … what will you use, and how will we get away with it?"

We all looked at each other and laughed. You see, friends will help you move, but girlfriends will help you move bodies. Friends will also bail you out of jail, but girlfriends will sit next to you in jail and say, "Wow, that was fun!"

Why Kathy jeopardized her friendship with Gina is still a mystery to us. Gina told everyone about Kathy and Nick's affair and about the abortion. She also told Kathy's mother. She never spoke to Kathy again. None of us did. Talk about *persona non grata*. She was history.

Kathy broke two very important rules:

1. Don't get paid and laid in the same place.
2. If your best friend's husband hits on you, tell him he's a pig, and then tell your best friend. (This works best when you tell her in front of him.)

I once had to follow my own advice: Rule No. 2. Years ago, after I ended a relationship with Rick, I heard a knock at the door late one night. It was almost 1:30 a.m., but I was awake. I was on the telephone talking with a girlfriend. I told her that someone was knocking on the door. She told me that she would wait while I checked who was at the door. Through the peephole, I could see that it was my friend Aaron. I had graduated from high school the same year as Aaron. We had known each other since the sixth grade. Not only that, Aaron and Rick worked together. They were good friends. Aaron's wife, Nancy, and I were also friends. So I was not concerned that he was at my house. I thought that he might be drunk and might need a ride home.

I opened the door and asked Aaron if he was okay. Aaron was holding a six-pack of beer in one hand. He asked me, "Do you want to have a few beers?"

I was a bit surprised. I wasn't sure if he was drunk. I told him that I did not want to drink, but that I could drive him home. He made no attempt to come into the house.

He said, "I'm just lonely, and I know you're lonely, too."

At that point, I said, "Aaron, I am not lonely. You need to leave. Don't ever do this to me again."

He nodded, but he did not say anything. He turned to leave. He took a few steps before turning around.

He said, "Don't tell Rick I was here, okay."

I said, "Okay, I won't tell him."

He returned to his car and drove away.

The next day, I could not stop thinking about what I should do. I was tormented about whether to tell Nancy or keep it to myself. I knew that if I told her, it was going to hurt her. At noon, I called Nancy at work.

I told her, "You know that I would never want to hurt you in any way."

She sounded concerned when she said, "I know."

Then I told her that Aaron had come to the house and what he had said. I told Nancy that I had only offered to take Aaron home because I thought he might be drunk. I was worried that he might hurt himself or someone else.

Nancy asked, "Do you mind if I mention this to Aaron?"

I said, "By all means, tell him that I called you."

That afternoon, Nancy called me at home. She told me that she had just talked to Aaron. She had confronted him with what I had told her earlier.

She said, "He's right here, and he wants to talk to you."

Aaron's voice came through the telephone. He said, "Hey, this is a big misunderstanding. I didn't ask you if you wanted to drink a beer with me. I told you I'd had a few beers. And I did not tell you that I was lonely. I told you that I was alone. You got it all wrong."

I told him, "You and I both know exactly what happened last night. If that's the explanation you want to give to Nancy, you still have to explain why you went to my house in the first place. You knew that I was alone and that Rick would not be there. Nancy knows that, too. Tell her the truth or I will call Rick and tell him you came to my house last night. I will tell him everything you said, and he will believe me. I'll call you back in ten minutes."

I didn't even have to wait the ten minutes. Nancy called me back a few minutes later and said, "He's busted. He said it happened just as you said. I think he's afraid you're going to tell Rick."

She didn't sound too upset.

I told her, "He knows that I would not tell Rick as long as he told you the truth."

Nancy said, "I believed you. I'm glad you told me."

We hung up. Aaron never pulled that stunt again, at least not with me.

I have always accepted that infidelity is a natural consequence to marriage. Don't get me wrong. It's a hard pill to swallow, but it happens in the best of marriages. While I don't condone this in any way, I recognize the fact that if the circumstances are perfect, a man will cheat on his wife. In fact, the circumstances don't have to be that perfect. Yes, that is scary!

I knew that the percentage of men who cheated on their wives was high. I logged on to the Internet and started looking for statistics on infidelity in marriages.

There weren't any good sites so I turned to my husband and asked him, "Honey, what percentage of men do you think cheat on their wives?"

As if he had been waiting for me to ask him that question, he answered, "One hundred."

I said, "Excuse me."

So he repeated, "One hundred percent."

I said, "Yes, I heard you. But you just included yourself?"

He said, "Me? How did I get involved in this? I was just trying to help you." Then he said, "If you are going to talk about men who cheat on their wives, you have to talk about women who cheat on their husbands." He continued, "What would you say if I caught you cheating on me?"

I thought about it for a moment before I said, "I would tell you that I just wanted to try it." Then I said, "If I thought you were still mad, I would go walk it off." He just shook his head. Sometimes, he has no sense of humor.

Where was I? Men do not cheat on their wives because they have stopped loving their wives. Most men who cheat on their wives have no intentions of leaving their wives. These men do not want to lose their families or their housekeeper. Many of the men who cheat believe they are not having sex with their partners as often as they want. They also believe they are not getting the kind of sex they want. Then, they justify their infidelity by blaming their wives for gaining weight, not being pretty anymore, and not appreciating them. I once asked a man if he cheated on his wife. He responded, "I don't cheat on my life."

I used to work with a man who had a reputation of cheating on his wife. One day, a very attractive woman walked into the office and he said, "Wow! I could leave my wife for her."

I asked him, "You would leave your wife for her?"

He responded, "Well, I would leave her for a couple of hours."

As much as men love their wives, they constantly fantasize about having sex with other women ... lots of women, hundreds of them, and the younger the better. One hundred percent, remember. Married or otherwise, men will always find other women attractive. If your husband or boyfriend tells you he is not attracted to other women, you should be very concerned. Not only would I question him, I would probably follow him.

I think we all wonder, "When is it fantasy and when is it cheating?" The answer is: When he forgets to tell you about her, it's cheating! If he tells her about you, and he touches her anyway, it's cheating!

When a man has an affair with a woman, everything changes. He does not just wake up one day and have an affair. First, he meets a woman whom he finds attractive. They casually develop an emotional bond, a friendship outside of his marriage. They decide to keep this friendship a secret between the two of them. The friendship inevitably becomes a sexual relationship. Then I find out and I kill them both. Then I go to prison because I could not prove an insanity plea. Okay, that did not turn out well.

So what's the alternative, you ask? You confront your fears. You tell your man that you understand his inherent need to have sex with other women. You explain to him that in the event he ever has the opportunity to have sex with another woman, you want to watch.

At this point, he will most likely ask, "What did you just say?"

He thinks he knows what you just said. He just never thought he would ever hear you say it. So you might have to repeat it. Tell him that he needs to invite you. The reactions vary, but most of them are first comical and then annoying. Most men will have this on their minds the rest of the day, and the next day, and the day after that. How will you know that? Because they will bring it up over and over and over and over. For most men, the only thing better than having sex with a woman is having sex with two women. This will just give him something different to think about for a while. He might even want to kick himself for not having thought about this before. All these years he was fantasizing about having sex with one woman. He could have been fantasizing about having sex with two women.

8.

Today Is Our What?

Ten Things Men Should Not Say on Their Wedding Anniversary

1. *Are we still doing that?*
2. *Anniversary? I made other plans with the guys.*
3. *I don't want to go to dinner. I want to watch the game.*
4. *You go celebrate with the kids.*
5. *Okay, but I want pizza.*
6. *I didn't get you a card; I can write you a note.*
7. *I'll go to dinner if you promise we'll have sex later.*
8. *I forgot; I thought it was next year.*
9. *I have a stomachache.*
10. *Today is our what?*

I found these terribly amusing. When I shared them with Jen, she said, "Five years ago, I would have found them amusing, too. Instead, I have one to add to your list."

She continued, "Mark and I had not celebrated our past five anniversaries. We married on December 20, just five days before

Christmas. Every year, we had huge family celebrations on Christmas Eve, Christmas Day, and New Year's Eve. However, we did nothing on the 20th. I could not understand why it was no big deal for Mark. I had no memory of the previous five anniversaries, not a single one. This anniversary, however, would be memorable.

"I came home at 4:00 p.m. I wished Mark a happy anniversary. Surprisingly, he came over and gave me a kiss and a hug. I told Mark that I had a dental appointment at 4:30 p.m., and I would be back by 6:00 p.m. I asked him if he wanted to have dinner, and he nodded. I had always bought Mark a special gift on our anniversary. Mark, on the other hand, had never given me any cards, gifts, or flowers on our past anniversaries. Nothing. At the very least, I would settle for dinner.

"By the time I returned home, Mark was gone. At 7:45 p.m., I called Mark's cellular telephone, and he said he was on his way home. I heard him drive up at 9:00 p.m. It was too late for dinner. At first, Mark tried to say that he had forgotten the time. The truth was that he had simply chosen to continue hanging out with his friends. Then, out of nowhere, he declared that no husbands liked celebrating their anniversaries. He said that men only celebrated anniversaries so their wives would let them go golfing or hunting and fishing. He said that he had never celebrated anniversaries, not even with his ex-wife. He went so far as to say that even his two brothers did not celebrate their anniversaries with their wives. Mark added that he could not recall his parents ever celebrating their wedding anniversary."

Jen admitted, "I knew all of this was true. Still, I would never understand how a day that was so important to me was completely meaningless to him. He was not even willing to try and pretend that it meant something.

"I knew that as long as I was married to Mark, we would not be celebrating our anniversary. I did not want to accept it. I would not accept it. I tried to explain my position. I went into detail about why it was important to me. I asked Mark if he was one day not going to celebrate my birthday, or Christmas, or Thanksgiving. These days were still important to him.

"Mark listened impatiently. When I was done, Mark said, 'Fine, we'll do something next year.' Yes, that's what he said, 'We'll do something next year.' I would have to wait an entire year. Not tomorrow, not this weekend, but next year. I stared at him and coldly said, 'But you're not going to be here next year.'

"I went to my bedroom, locked it, and went to bed. The next day, I did the same thing. I could not even stand to look at him. Mark knew that I had made numerous concessions in our marriage. Not this time. Mark needed to understand that it was in his best interest to concede to my demands. It was a demand, and he was going to learn to enjoy it."

Jen chuckled a little before she continued. "I did not speak to Mark for five days. I left the house early in the morning. I came home and ate my dinner in the bedroom. I read my book, watched television, and made telephone calls, all from the comforts of my wonderful bedroom. I was beginning to believe that I could live here forever. On the sixth day, I came home to find a note on the front door. I was afraid to read it. The note read, 'YOU WIN.' What did that mean? 'You win, I want a divorce.' 'You win, I'm leaving you.' I entered my house cautiously. There was a single rose on the counter, next to three chocolate kisses. Mark was sitting on the couch and dressed like he was going to a job interview. He said, 'I thought you might want to go out and celebrate.' Even as he said it, I wanted him to add, 'our wedding anniversary.' I simply said, 'Thank you.' We went out and had a wonderful dinner. We talked about the last five days. Mark said that he realized I was not going to budge when I moved a small refrigerator into the bedroom."

Men also seem to either forget or ignore birthdays. Even when a woman reminds her husband that her birthday is a week or two away, he somehow forgets anyway. Although a woman will get telephone calls from her parents, her siblings, and all of her friends all day long, he still manages to forget. A man may even become indifferent to his wife's birthday and other special events. It appears that the more important the event is to her, the more indifferent he chooses to be.

Sofia confided that last year her usually thoughtful husband seemed to quit caring about her when it came to special events. She confided,

"It began with our wedding anniversary on November 12. Although money was tight, I purchased a simple but meaningful gift for Ronnie. After I presented him with the gift, Ronnie said, 'I thought we weren't getting each other anything. We're so tight on money. I didn't get you anything.' I responded, 'It's okay. I just did not want to let it go by,' referring to our anniversary. On Christmas Eve, Ronnie and I went to my in-laws for the yearly Christmas gift exchange party. While everyone was exchanging gifts, I presented my gift to Ronnie. It was not a part of the gift exchange. Ronnie was surprised. It was a DVD/VCR combo that was on his wish list. He looked embarrassed when he whispered, 'I thought we were only doing the gift exchange. I didn't get you anything.' Throughout our marriage, he had always bought me a Christmas gift. This year, he had no gift for me. I was so hurt, but I let it pass. On Valentine's Day, I bought Ronnie a card and some fishing lures. After I gave him the card and the gift, he ran to the grocery store to pick up some steaks for dinner. While he was there, he picked up a small bouquet of flowers and a card. He didn't write my name on the envelope. He signed the card, 'Ronnie.'

"In April, I was celebrating a birthday. The day before my birthday, my sister Veronica flew in from Mexico so she could celebrate with me. On my birthday around noon, Ronnie found time to say, 'Happy Birthday.' However, he made no mention of any plans he might have to celebrate in the evening. The following morning, I was participating in a bike ride in a city which was fifty miles away. On the afternoon of my birthday, we packed our things, and drove fifty miles and found a hotel near the starting point. On the evening of my birthday, we went to dinner only because it was dinnertime. Ronnie made no mention of my birthday. He balked when I said I wanted to order dessert. The following weekend, I asked Ronnie if we could have friends and family over for a cookout to celebrate my birthday. He said, 'No.' I kept insisting that we should have at least celebrated my birthday with a cake. He asked, 'What for?' About a week later, we were at the grocery store and I saw two birthday cakes. One of the cakes was tall and round, but small. The other cake was flat with lots of frosting. I preferred the tall and round cake. Ronnie, who loves frosting, preferred the other cake. We could not agree on which cake to purchase. I thought it was up to me to choose, so I asked him jokingly, 'Whose birthday was it?' Ronnie snapped, 'Fine, but you better eat it all.' Needless to say, we did not take either cake. As we left the store, Ronnie noticed that I was crying. He asked, 'Why didn't you take the cake?' He added, 'I told you to take it if you wanted it.' There was no point. I had to accept the fact that he just did not want or care to celebrate my birthday."

Sofia continued, "A few months later, we were at my sister Rose's house. Ronnie began to tell us a story about his best friend, Simon, and Simon's wife, Crystal. Apparently, during a recent business trip out of town, Ronnie had stayed with Simon and Crystal for a week. This coincided with Simon's birthday. Ronnie was upset that Crystal had been indifferent about celebrating Simon's birthday. Ronnie could not understand why Crystal did not want to make any effort to celebrate his best friend's birthday. Ronnie questioned, 'How can she be like that?' and 'Can you believe it? She didn't want to do anything for him.' Rose was also puzzled about why Crystal would not want to celebrate her husband's birthday. She went so far as to say, 'Maybe she doesn't love him.' At this point, Ronnie bragged to us that he had convinced Crystal to get a babysitter so they could all go out to dinner. Ronnie even mentioned that he had covered the tab for dinner and drinks. It sounded like they had all had a great time. He was very proud of himself for being such a great friend. I wondered if they ordered cake for dessert. I was sure they had. I let Ronnie finish describing how a meaningless birthday turned out to be a wonderful evening. He took all the credit.

"When he was finished, I turned to Ronnie and said, 'Wow. How could she be like that? But, wait a minute. This whole scenario sounds very familiar to me. Didn't something like this happen to me a couple of months ago?' Ronnie knew exactly what I was talking about. He didn't say another word. Rose asked, 'What do you mean? What happened?' When she saw the look on Ronnie's face, she quit asking. I, however, felt obligated to explain to my sister that I was still waiting for Ronnie to consider celebrating my birthday. I told her I would have settled for a cake of my choosing and celebrating with my husband and children in the privacy of our home. It was a very quiet and uncomfortable moment for all of us. But, I felt justified in pointing out that while Ronnie might be a great friend, he had not been a very caring husband under similar circumstances." Touché!

Sofia noted, "A few weeks ago, Ronnie asked me what I wanted for our anniversary. My first thought was that I wanted a very big apology. Instead, I told Ronnie that I would think about it and let him know. It was very nice of him to ask. I told him that I wanted a CD or a DVD. I was happy that I would not get a repeat of last year. However, the anniversary came and went, and I got nothing."

If celebrating wedding anniversaries, birthdays, and other special events is very important to you, make sure you resolve this before you decide to get married. If you are already married to a man who does not celebrate wedding anniversaries or birthdays, you have to decide if you can live with that. He is not going to wake up one day, bring you flowers, make dinner reservations, and say, "Happy anniversary, my darling" or "Happy birthday, sweetheart." It is not going to happen. Even if you can somehow cajole him into celebrating, he is going to express his extreme displeasure at being forced to do this. Think very hard about how important this is to you. If this is a necessary part of your marriage, you could always get married again. Otherwise, you might just have to live with it.

9.

Guy@homewatchingsports.com

On their wedding day, the groom did not show up. After waiting for an hour, the bride and her entourage drove to the golf course, where they found the groom playing golf in his tuxedo. In his defense, the groom said, "I told you that if it rained, we'd get married on Saturday."

—*Unknown*

Initially, I left this entire section blank. I thought the title was self-explanatory, and it needed nothing. However, this is a sore subject for many women. The reality is that men spend (waste) a massive amount of time watching sports, especially on television. The biggest dilemma for women is that there are sports year-round. They never stop. There are football games on Sunday and Monday nights. Baseball games, it seems, are on all the time. There are also a number of hockey and basketball games. And all of these sports have playoffs, which last for days, even weeks. Then there is golf on Sunday. Typically, men will play golf on Sunday morning. Then, they watch golf on television the rest of the afternoon. Most men are not good enough to play golf, but they call it that anyway. Men will also find time to play golf during the week, usually after work. Then, they come home to watch some game on television. It is endless. The following week, it starts all over again.

A few years ago, my husband's brother, Guy, and his wife, Juanita, moved to a new home. Juanita called to give us their new telephone number, home address, and email address. She mentioned that when they set up their Internet service, the technician told her that their temporary email address was *Guy@home.com*. On an impulse, Juanita asked the technician if she could change the email address to *Guy@homewatchingsports.com*. I don't know if Guy thought this was funny. I thought it was hilarious. There is no question that Guy watches a lot of sports on television. He even has the baseball channel.

My husband also watches a lot of sports like baseball, hockey, tennis, golf, and some basketball games. More than anything, he loves baseball. Once, when we were still living in Idaho, we took a short vacation to Wyoming and Montana. I had almost forgotten it was baseball season. After a long day at Yellowstone National Park, we drove north into Gardiner, Montana, and checked into a hotel room overlooking the Yellowstone River. It was a beautiful location.

Immediately after we brought our things into the room, my husband announced, "I guess I am going to have to go to one of the local bars in town since you girls are not going to want to watch the game."

I asked him, "What game?"

He almost shouted, "The Series is on."

Then I remembered that the World Series of baseball was still on. I asked, "When does the game start?"

He answered, "In five minutes."

I had wanted to walk down to the river. I had wanted to have a nice dinner at one of the local restaurants. I had wanted all three of us to go as a family. I was so disappointed. I found my purse and motioned for my daughter to come with me.

I turned to my husband and said, "We'll see you later. Do you know how to get back to Boise?"

Without responding to my question, he said, "Just leave her here. She doesn't have to go."

He only wanted Lisa to stay with him to ensure that I would return. I decided to just let it go. The game would be over sooner or later. Besides, I had other things I needed to do. I told him, "Go ahead and watch the game here. Lisa can watch a movie on her DVD player. I'll go get dinner."

He said, "Okay."

I love taking charge. Even as I walked out of the room, I could not help but shake my head.

When it comes to sports, my husband is like most men. They love sports. I believe that most women will agree that their boyfriends or husbands watch a lot of sports on television. I just do not get it. After all, the news and sports channels always show the highlights of each game. I do not hate sports. But other than gymnastics or tennis, I would just rather see the highlights or sports bloopers. The Olympic Games are always fun to watch, and they only come every four years. I can handle that. I also enjoy watching sports programs that spotlight particular athletes. The rest seems like such a waste of time.

I have tried watching baseball games with my husband. But, he does not make it any fun. He has rules. Rule number one is that I have to be quiet. Rule number two is that I have to be still. Rule number three is that if I cannot be quiet and I cannot be still, I have to move to the don't-bother-me couch. I hate that couch. The problem is that my husband has no patience with me. I have lots of questions during the game, most of which he refuses to acknowledge, much less answer. I am just curious. I mean, has anyone ever wondered …

1. Do you think the baseball uniforms are made out of polyester?
2. Do the players have to wash their own uniforms?
3. How many games do you have to watch before you become an athletic supporter?
4. Do the "cups" come in different sizes?
5. Do the players lie about their cup size?
6. Is crying allowed in baseball?

7. Do the players get the sunflower seeds for free?
8. If a player makes $5,000,000 per year, does he have direct deposit?
9. Does he get twelve equal monthly payments of $416,666.66?
10. Do the dugouts have air conditioning?
11. If a player wants a hotdog, will someone bring it to him?
12. Does he have to pay for it?
13. Does he get a discount?

When he completely ignores me, I ask him, "Honey, do you want to make love during the commercial?" Game Over!

I have to tell you that if I had a dollar for every game or sporting event my husband watched on television, I would not have to write this book. Actually, I have learned a lot of things from watching sports. For example, I have learned:

1. The players do not wear outfits; they wear uniforms.
2. Four minutes left in the game is equal to at least half an hour real time.
3. For the most part, there is nothing sexual about patting another player on the butt in any sport.
4. "Rearranging" is normal, like breathing.
5. Spitting gobs of phlegm is also like breathing, but more like exhaling.
6. In golf, you cannot make the holes larger, and you cannot add more holes to choose from; you just can't.
7. In any sport, everyone knows that Michael Jordan is a gift from God.
8. Hockey players are the toughest players in the world, but they don't bite.
9. Removing or blocking the sports channel is grounds for divorce.
10. Winning is everything!

Aside from watching sports on television, my husband is an avid bow-hunter. Hunting is his passion. I have a confession to make. In 1996, I moved to Alaska so that my husband could go hunting full-time. When I married him, I was aware that he was attempting to "harvest" the twenty-seven North American big game animals with a bow and arrow. Of the twenty-seven animals, fourteen of the species he needed to harvest could be found in Alaska and in Canada. At the time, only five men in the world had ever accomplished this incredible feat.

I left my family, my friends, my home, and my job. My friends all thought I was crazy. My mother thought it was a chance for a wonderful adventure.

My father said, "Just remember, you're only as far as your MasterCard."

That was my cue that I could come home anytime.

We packed our belongings into a travel trailer, which we hitched to our truck. Geographically, I did not even know exactly where Alaska was or just how far north it was from the continental United States. Still, I felt both terrified and exhilarated at the thought of this great adventure. It took us ten days to get to Alaska. I had begun to think that we would never get there, but we did.

I would not encourage any woman to drop everything and move to Alaska as I did. Mine was an extreme situation. Most men just want to play golf on the weekend—every weekend. Some of them plan weeklong hunting trips or fishing trips with their buddies. A week before the trip, they still have not told their wives about the trip. To resolve this problem, they stage an argument or they find a reason to be mad at their wives. Now, they can pack their stuff and leave on their trip without feeling any guilt or remorse.

Nicole became visibly upset when she told me her "fishing" story. Nicole said, "Ben and I had been married for less than two years. In early July 1992, I gave birth to twin boys. It was the happiest time of my life. Yet, I had never been so completely exhausted. In mid-August, I overheard Ben talking on the telephone with his best friend, Paul, about a fishing trip to Alaska. When I asked Ben if he was planning a fishing trip, he said that he was not. He said that Paul and his brother, Chuck, were going fishing in Alaska for two weeks. For years, Ben had either gone hunting or fishing with Paul and Chuck, usually during the month of September. Ben said that he wanted to go, but he had told Paul that he did not think I would let him go. I was a bit upset at Ben for blaming me for not being able to go. I wished that Ben would have told Paul that he needed to stay and help me with the twins."

Nicole continued her story. "I thought nothing of it when Ben told me that he was going to take some fishing equipment to Paul. Ben had left early in the morning. He never came back. Early in the afternoon, I called Paul to see if Ben was still there. There was no answer. By late afternoon, I knew that Ben had gone to Alaska with Paul and Chuck. I went to the garage and I could not locate any of Ben's fishing gear. It was gone. I checked Ben's closet and I noticed that some of his clothes were gone as well. As upset as I was, I turned my attention to my children. I needed to shake this off and take care of them.

"Ben had taken the truck, and it was the only vehicle we had. I didn't know if Ben had left it at Paul's house or parked it at the airport. Ben called later that night to say that he was in Seattle, on his way to Alaska. He mentioned that the truck was at Paul's house. He offered no explanations or apologies. He said he just wanted me to know where he was. He told me that I would never understand that he had to go on this trip as he had every year. He said he would be back in two weeks. I was still on maternity leave, so I did not have to go to work. In any event, I needed a vehicle to get around. The next day, I called one of my friends and asked her to take me to Paul's house to pick up the truck. I called a friend because I was too embarrassed to say anything to my parents or to anyone else. When I finally told my parents, I broke down and cried for a long time. My parents were furious with Ben for putting me through this. This was the beginning of the end of our marriage. We stayed married for another five years, but it was never the same. It got to the point where I could not even hear the word 'fishing' without getting angry. He had left me at the worst possible time in my life, and he never offered an apology. He didn't have one."

What would possess a man to sneak his clothes and his fishing gear out of his home and leave his wife and newborn babies to go fishing for two weeks? If you don't know, mark this page, close the book, and read the title again.

10.

Sexhausted

A middle-aged woman was sitting in a bar enjoying a drink with her girlfriends when a handsome and sexy young man entered the bar. The woman could not help but stare. The man noticed and walked directly toward her.

He leaned over and whispered to her, "I'll do anything, absolutely anything, that you want me to do, no matter how wild or kinky, for $100, on one condition. You have to tell me in three words."

The woman considered his proposition for a moment, and then slowly removed a $100 bill from her purse. She pressed the money into the young man's hand along with her address and whispered, "Clean my house."

—*Unknown*

Do you remember what the sex was like in the beginning? It was great! So what happened? Do women's sexual urges wane after they get married? I don't think so. It is not that women lose interest in sex. Women certainly enjoy sex as much as men do. For the most part, women are simply exhausted. They do not get enough sleep. They do not have enough hours in the day to do everything that they need to accomplish every day. That is because most women have full-time jobs, and then they come home to finish the housework and care for the children. Essentially, women have two full-time jobs.

My friend Valeria's biggest complaint when she was married was that she felt like a single mother. Her now ex-husband Greg did little to help her at home. He was oblivious to her needs and the needs of their children. Needless to say, their sex life suffered.

She said, "I got home from work only to begin my second full-time job. I had so many things to do, and I was completely overwhelmed. My day job wasn't this hard. Greg used to sit on the couch and watch television. He got off the couch only to eat dinner, to use the bathroom, to take a shower, and to go to bed. Whenever I asked him if he could help me with dinner or if I mentioned that I needed his help with some laundry, he would snarl at me and say, 'You can't stand letting me relax because you have to clean the house.' I don't know if he noticed everything that I did all night long. I don't know if he realized that I was exhausted. By the time I was ready for sleep, he was ready for sex. I was ready to tell him to go #*&% himself."

In some relationships, men come to believe that it is a woman's duty to please them sexually. These men are not concerned about whether women achieve any sexual gratification. Often, these men make sexual demands that women find uncomfortable. Some demands can be painful, not to mention humiliating and embarrassing. Sometimes, men threaten to go to a prostitute if their wives refuse to meet their demands. It is also not uncommon for a man to brag that an ex-girlfriend or an ex-wife "used to do it all the time, and she loved it." I don't think so. I'll bet if you asked the ex-girlfriend or the ex-wife, she'd tell you, "He used to try that on me all the time. Don't believe him and don't worry. He's too cheap to hire a prostitute." You do not have to do anything that makes you uncomfortable. Next time he wants to sodomize you, tell him, "You first." However, don't be surprised if he says okay.

Some men want you to act like a prostitute in the bedroom, but they expect you to be prim and proper everywhere else. Years ago, my friend

Bonnie traveled to Colorado one summer for a weeklong conference. At the conference, she met and fell in love with Carl. Bonnie was from Texas. She had four older brothers, who were all cowboys. Carl was from Georgia. He was an only child, whose parents were both ministers. Bonnie and Carl spent the entire week together. After the conference ended, Bonnie returned to Texas and Carl returned to Georgia. Over the next several months, Carl traveled several times to Texas to be with Bonnie. He even spent Thanksgiving with Bonnie, where he met Bonnie's family. At Christmas, Bonnie traveled to Georgia to meet Carl's parents.

Immediately after Carl picked up Bonnie at the airport, he said to her, "I don't know if you know it or not, but you do curse a lot. So I would appreciate it if you don't swear in front of my family."

Bonnie was fully aware that she used a lot of profanity. Still, she felt herself getting defensive, so she tried to be calm. Skipping her favorite four-letter word, she asked Carl, "What is wrong with the way I talk?"

In a smug manner, Carl answered, "Well, Bonnie, it is just not very ladylike."

Bonnie said, "Really. Well, neither is a blow job, and you didn't say anything about that."

After she finished her story, Bonnie told me, "It was at that exact moment that I took a good look at Carl. I did not know what I had seen in him. It must have been the Colorado mountain air."

Sometimes, women do not want to have sex. Sometimes, women cannot have sex. When a woman is on her period, she does not want to have sex. The first tampon wrapper a man sees in the garbage, he acts like it is the end of the world. He mopes and sulks, and keeps asking, "Are you done yet?" Listen, buddy, this isn't a road trip. Having a period is no picnic. Women hate having periods. From the time we are barely teenagers, we have a period, month after month after month.

What is amazing is that men view this as a huge inconvenience to THEM. I have news for these men. Women hate the words "tampon," "maxi-pads," "mini-pads," "PMS," and "wings." I, for one, would like to see a man place a thick, cotton pad between his legs and try to walk around with it … for seven days! Maybe then, men would stop asking, "Is Aunt Flow visiting?" Some men even refuse to cuddle with their wives or girlfriends during this time. Men treat women as though they are broken or something. What men don't stop to realize is that sex during this time of the month does not have to be interrupted. Men just need to be willing to go outside the box. Instead of always thinking penetration, they could start thinking ejaculation. It should not matter how they achieve this, as long as they do. Next time he makes a comment about you being on your period, show him your hands and say, "I may be broken, but I still have these. So, be nice to me."

11.
Say It with Me: Laundry

A woman took her husband to the emergency room after he complained about chest pains. The man was released after a checkup, but the doctor asked to speak privately to the wife.

The doctor said, "Your husband is suffering from a very severe stress disorder. If you don't follow my instructions carefully, your husband will die." The doctor then gave her a list of written instructions.

1. *Prepare three healthy and nutritious meals every day.*
2. *Be pleasant and responsive at all times.*
3. *Do not ask him to do chores or tasks.*
4. *Do not put him through unnecessary stress.*

After the wife read the instructions, the doctor said, "If you can do this, I believe your husband will regain his health completely within the year."

On the way home, the husband asked his wife, "What did the doctor say to you?"

The wife replied, "He said you're going to die."

—Unknown

The process to donate a kidney to my father began in the summer of 2002. A week after submitting some blood for testing, I found out that my father and I matched perfectly. The hard part was selling my father on the idea that he should take one of my kidneys. The alternative was for him to remain on the national waiting list. He would die first.

I could not keep this a secret from my husband, for too long, anyway. One day, he picked up the mail and found a booklet that the transplant center had sent. When I came home from work, he asked me why the transplant center was sending me information. He already knew because he knew that my father had been on kidney dialysis for the past year. I tried to explain to my husband that I was going to give my father one of my kidneys. I told him the transplant center had sent me a booklet that contained information about the donor's surgery. It was a Q&A for him to read. He was furious.

He stormed out of the house, but not before saying, "I forbid you to do this."

Well, that went in one ear and out the other. This was my father, and I did not need my husband's permission to save my father's life.

He came back home after he calmed down, if I can call it that. He was not happy at all. It was not as though I had done anything wrong. I tried to give him the booklet, but he would not take it. I placed it on the coffee table. I started surfing the Internet, looking for photographs of the hotel where we were going to stay before and after the transplant. I was also looking for nearby attractions and restaurants, and where the biggest mall was located. You know, priorities.

I looked back and saw that my husband was reading the information in the booklet.

Suddenly, he asked, "What are we supposed to do if something happens to you?"

I walked over and sat on the coffee table and said, "Well, you will just have to hire a maid. But you are going to have to pay that one."

I laughed, and he snickered. He did not ask any more questions.

On November 2, 2002, I traveled to Texas for the surgery. I was in Texas for sixteen days. Both operations were a complete success. I have to be honest. The pain during the first few days was excruciating. I even had my own personal morphine pump. That's something you don't see every day. After the second day, I felt well enough to go see my father. I asked my nurse if she could take me. It took us about fifteen minutes just to walk across the hall. I walked in and found my father sitting up in his hospital bed. He had a tray of hospital food, and he was eating heartily. He was watching the news on television and he looked great!

I was released from the hospital four days after my surgery. My father was required to stay for another week. He just looked better by the day. My mother and I stayed at the hotel. We went to the hospital every day until my father was released. We stayed for a few more days to keep a doctor's appointment. I was then able to drive the five-hour trek back to my parents' home, taking only over-the-counter pain meds. A few days later, I headed back to Idaho. I wanted and needed my mother or my sister to come back with me. However, my mother had to take care of my father, and my sister had to work. Still, I was grateful that I had a husband and a daughter who were waiting for me. They would take care of me.

My husband and daughter picked me up at the airport. They were both very careful with me, not wanting to hurt me in any way. It was great to be home. I did not have to work the following day, but my daughter had to go to school. I went to her closet to get her clothes ready for the next day. I found that most of her clothes were gone. The only clothes left hanging in her closet were some short-sleeve shirts. It was November, and it was already chilly in Idaho.

I went back to my bedroom and asked my husband, "Where are all of Lisa's clothes?"

He said, "I don't know. I guess she grew out of everything."

I thought to myself, "I was only gone for sixteen days. She could not have outgrown her clothes in that time."

I checked the dirty laundry hamper and lo and behold … I pulled out Lisa's long-sleeve shirts, counting them out loud as I tossed them at Ken. The rest of her clothes and my husband's clothes were in there, too. There was sixteen days' worth of laundry in the hamper.

I asked him, "Why didn't you do the laundry?"

He responded, "Because we never ran out of clean clothes."

I remember telling my friend Connie that story. She had a huge complaint about her husband, Oscar. She told me, "I used to ask Oscar if he could do at least one load of laundry. He could not understand why I needed him to do any laundry at all. He said, 'It's not like you are actually washing the clothes. The machine washes it.'"

Connie looked at me and said, "I did not bother to explain to him that doing laundry is not that simple. There are a number of things that I have to do before I do the laundry. I first have to look around the entire house for dirty clothes that the kids and Oscar forget to place in the hamper. That means I have to look under and behind all of the beds, in all of the closets, in the garage, and inside Oscar's truck and my car. Then I gather all of the laundry and bring it to the laundry room. Sometimes, this takes three or four trips. The huge pile of clothes equals several loads that I separate into whites, colors, jeans, towels, and delicates (mine). One load at a time, I place the clothes in the washer, then set the water level, wash/rinse temperature, set for regular fabrics, wrinkle-free, or delicates, and add the detergent. Once the first load is washed, I take out the clothes from the washer and place them in the dryer, along with a dryer sheet. Then I place another load of clothes in the washer, set the water level, wash/rinse temperature, etc., etc., etc.

"This is just the beginning. Once each load of laundry is dry, I have to sort the clothes. I fold what needs to be folded and hang on hangers what needs to be on hangers. Then I have to put it all away. The worst part is that even before I finish doing the laundry, there are more clothes in the hamper." Connie looked so depressed. She turned to me and said, "Tell me again why I got married and had children."

Laundry is but one part of housework. There are beds to make, floors to sweep and mop, toilets to scrub, carpets to vacuum, and everyone's favorite … dusting. In the kitchen, the dishes have to be washed. Even if you have a dishwasher, the dishes have to be loaded and unloaded. Incidentally, the word "wife" is not synonymous with the word "dishwasher." Additionally, the counters and appliances have to be wiped down.

At the very least, women do twice as much housework as men. Women do most of the routine tasks such as cleaning and cooking. In most households, there is very little in the way of sharing of the household chores. This leads to feelings of unfairness and exploitation. It also leads to a great many arguments, most of which women start with, "You are a lazy, disgusting pig."

There is no question that women are multi-task oriented. Women can cook dinner, help with homework, wash laundry, watch a television show, and carry on a telephone conversation, all at the same time.

Men, on the other hand, are single-task oriented. Using the remote control, they can flip through the channels. They cannot flip through the channels and answer a ringing telephone or doorbell. They cannot flip through the channels and tell a screaming child to be quiet. However, I must say that things are changing every day. I recently saw a man put the remote control down and lift up his feet so his wife could vacuum on that spot. If you are serious about getting your husband to help you with the housework, convince him that it is a sport. You can start by calling the clothes hamper a laundry basket. Tell him he will earn two points for every piece of clothing he throws and makes into the laundry basket. Be creative. It just has to sound like a sport.

12.

If I Had a Wife Instead of a Husband...

Men are like handguns. If you keep one around long enough, you are going to want to shoot it.

—Unknown

When I was still living in Alaska, my girlfriend Rachel called one day to let me know that the house next door to hers was for sale. We quickly came up with the idea that my husband and I could buy the house. Then my husband and her husband would live in that house. Rachel, her cats, my daughter, and I would live in her house. We realized that what we needed was a wife, not a husband. Wow! I could have a wife of my very own. It certainly had never occurred to her or me. That was the answer to all of our problems. It was an idea women all over the world would embrace. We even considered designing a Web site called *www.Ineedawife.com*. We started brainstorming and making a list of our ideas. It would be revolutionary. However, it occurred to us that as soon as men found the Web site, they would think it was a way for them to meet women.

Still, I could not help wondering how women would complete the statement "If I had a wife instead of a husband ..." I received the following responses from my girlfriends:

1. I would give a hug without having sex.
2. I would get flowers more often.
3. I would have only two children, instead of three.
4. I would have someone ask me what I wanted for dinner.
5. I would have an orgasm EVERY time.
6. I would have help around the house.
7. I would get a cup of tea without asking.
8. I would receive my presents wrapped, not in a grocery bag.
9. I would get pampered when I got sick.
10. I would experience the perks of having a wife: a clean home, cooked meals, child-rearing, sharing the finances/bills of the home, organization in the home, etc.
11. I would feel truly equal to my partner, not submissive or less of a person.
12. I would have someone help clean the house.
13. I would have someone who understands the need for talking, cuddling, mood swings, romance, etc.
14. Words like "bitch" and "nag" would never be used.
15. Shopping would be an all-day event.
16. Sports and sports channels would be on parental control.
17. I would have someone who remembered our anniversary.
18. I would have someone who made me a birthday cake.
19. Shopping excursions would replace marriage counseling.
20. I wouldn't have to fake it anymore.
21. And as only Marilyn could say, "I just wish I was married to me."

Women have two full-time jobs. This is a fact. We work all day long, skip our breaks, and take one hour for lunch. We typically use our lunch hours to run errands. When we get home from work, we might have a half-hour to ourselves before we cook dinner, wash one or two loads of laundry, vacuum, clean at least one bathroom, help with schoolwork, wash the dishes, clean the counters, put away the laundry, iron clothes for work the next day, and if we have time, sweep the patio.

So where are the husbands? You know where they are. If they are even home, they are busy watching television. The only time they get up is to eat their dinner. Half of them come to the kitchen for their plate of food, which they take back to the TV room to watch the game.

While it can be nice to be a wife, it is even nicer to have a wife. Put that on your Christmas wish list!

13.

Recipe for a Great Fruit Salad

A man and his wife were dining at a local restaurant. The husband kept looking at a woman sitting at a table nearby. She appeared to be intoxicated.

The wife asked her husband, "Do you know her?"

"Yes," the husband sighed. "She's my ex-wife. She started drinking right after we divorced seven years ago. I hear she hasn't been sober since."

The wife remarked, "Wow! She's been celebrating that long?"

—*Unknown*

A few days before Christmas one year, my husband noticed that I was making a menu for Christmas dinner. He came over and looked at the list.

He said, "What are we having for dessert?"

I said, "I don't know. I could bake a pie. Did you want me to make something?"

He said, "We could make a fruit salad, with whipped cream and stuff like that."

I thought to myself, "Fruit salad, I don't make fruit salad." I remembered that my husband's ex-wife is famous for her fruit salad.

I quickly dialed her telephone number. When she answered, I asked her, "Are you busy?"

She recognized my voice and asked, "What's up?"

I asked her, "Guess who misses your fruit salad. Can I have your recipe?"

She said, "Sure. It's an easy recipe. There is nothing to it."

She gave me a list of the ingredients, which I wrote down on a piece of paper. She then told me how to put it together. She also told me to call her back if I needed any help. Pretty amazing, huh?

I have always told my friends that I truly admire my husband's ex-wife. He certainly was lucky to be married to her. She is a good person. She was good to my husband when she was married to him. I wonder if he ever appreciated her for that.

I wish I could be more like her. Unfortunately, I am just the opposite. I know I am difficult to live with. I can be very demanding and controlling, and I don't like to let anything slide.

The first year that I dated my husband was tough on my husband's ex-wife. As happy as I was, I could not shake the feeling that my happiness was contingent upon her unhappiness. I knew that if I was going to marry this man, his ex-wife and their son were always going to be a part of his life, too. I could either choose to be friends with her or not. For me, the answer was easy. I wanted to be friends with her, but would she?

I did not know very much about her. What I did know was that she was a good person. I knew that because Ken was married to her for seventeen years, and they had known each other longer than that. If I was to believe that Ken was a good man, I had to believe that he would have only been married to a good woman.

I knew that I was eventually going to run into her somewhere. We would most likely find it awkward, and we would both pretend not to see each other. Instead, I decided to call her. None of my friends thought it was a good idea to call her. Everyone strongly discouraged me to do so.

Still, I knew that the worst possible thing that she could do was hang up on me. I could handle that. But that did not happen. One afternoon, I picked up the telephone and called her. We talked for about two hours. She was terrific! We made some promises to each other, and we vowed to keep them. I wanted her to know that, as long as I was married to Ken, his obligation to her and their son would never end.

They had known each other since junior high school. They married when they were still in high school. She was always going to be a part of his life, especially because they had a son together. We agreed that their son was the most important consideration. If their son knew that his mother and I were nice to each other, and that we liked each other, it would have a positive effect on him. He might even come to accept me. That was very important to me.

As time passed, I was most impressed by how well she and I got along. I was also pleasantly surprised at how much I liked her. We invited each other to dinner. We went to basketball games together and saved each other seats. We saw each other at Thanksgiving and Christmas. It worked out great. For me, she was the single most important person who helped me to understand my husband.

There were times when I called and asked her, "What is up with your freakin' husband?"

She calmly asked, "What did he do now?"

Of course, she and I caused some of our family members a bit of anxiety. My girlfriends and my family questioned my motives for being friendly with my husband's ex-wife. Her family was concerned that she might get hurt. She and I brushed off the concerns. However, there were others who did not like the fact that she and I could be friends. Some of these people even asked how I could be friendly with her. But, they were also going to her and asking her the same thing about me. You know those types of people, two-faced backstabbers who feed on chaos and thrive on misery and destruction. Geez, don't get me started. Luckily, she and I fully understood that there were some people who had no interest in us being friends and getting along. To this day, I strongly believe that if she and I were at each other's throats, it would only serve as a source of entertainment to others. We both vowed that we would never let that happen. We would never give anyone that satisfaction. Never! Nevertheless, they tried.

When we were living in Alaska, my husband flew to Texas after his father was hospitalized. One evening, he called from his ex-wife's house. She had just built her new home, and she had invited her family over for a party. Her parents, her sisters and their husbands, her nieces and nephews, along with her son and his then girlfriend, now wife, were all there. A few minutes after we hung up, I got another telephone call.

This time it was from a "concerned" family member, who said, "I hope this does not upset you. I thought you should know that, as we speak, your husband is at his ex-wife's house. You should call over there and get him out of there. You never know. He could end up spending the night with her, and you would never find out."

Of course, I did not let on that I knew he was at her house. I simply responded, "Listen, he had sex with her for over seventeen years; one more time is not going to hurt him." There was an audible gasp on the other end. I ended the telephone call.

I did not believe that he was going to spend the night with his ex-wife. I would not have been concerned if he had spent the night with his ex-wife. I knew that my husband was still a very big part of her and her family's lives. They all love him, and they will continue to love him. He loves them, too, and he should. They have been a part of his life now for more than thirty years. While I cannot begin to compete with the history between them, I can only hope to create my own history, which will always include them.

Sadly, this arrangement is the exception, rather than the rule. Typically, the ex-wife and the new girlfriend, or new wife, do not get along. Do you want to know why? There is nothing in it for the man. Since the ex-wife and the new girlfriend, or new wife, usually do not already know each other, this leaves a blank slate. A man gets to dictate what each of them learns about one another. When the new wife says she doesn't like the ex-wife, her reasons are most likely related to what she learned about the ex-wife from her husband. At least in the beginning, the new wife is going to believe all of the crap that her husband feeds her about his ex-wife. I cannot emphasize enough how important it is for the two women to talk to each other. The new wife might be surprised to learn what kinds of things her husband has said about her to his ex-wife as well. Do not forget that the ex-wife was his confidante for a long time. He feels comfortable sharing things with his ex-wife. He can be himself with his ex-wife in a way that the new girlfriend or new wife has yet to experience.

He also does not want his ex-wife and the new girlfriend or new wife to share stories about him. Believe me, these two women need to know the stories. The stories can mean the difference between getting to know him now and finding out years later what kind of a man he is.

Before I forget, I have to mention that some men never want to give up what they consider their back-up sex partners. Come to think of it, this is probably the most important reason why men do not want the ex-wives and new wives to get along.

Years ago, I traveled with a co-worker to an out-of-town conference. I knew Joe was remarried. He and his new wife had a one-year-old daughter. He also had two sons from his previous marriage. Since I was driving my car to the airport, which was forty-five miles away, Joe's new wife dropped him off at my house. On the drive to the airport, Joe seemed amused about something. He explained that on his way to my house, his wife had warned him not to be "messing around." By the time we arrived at our destination, Joe had disclosed a very intimate part of his life. He first said that his new wife had been his mistress for ten years. His mistress had continuously pestered him to leave his wife. Not only did he not want to leave his wife, he could not leave his wife. She was very religious, and she came from a very traditional family. He also did not have any reason to leave his wife. She was a faithful and dutiful wife, and she had done nothing wrong. Throughout their marriage, Joe's wife knew about his past affairs. She knew the names of Joe's mistresses. She knew where he was sleeping when he did not come home some nights.

Joe's mistress continued to pester him about getting a divorce. However, after ten years, she came to the realization that Joe would never leave his wife. She decided to move away and begin a new life. Joe was devastated. He realized that he loved his mistress, and he promised to divorce his wife. Two years later, he had not only married his mistress, but he and his new wife had a new baby.

The twist to this story was about to be revealed. He showed me a key and asked me, "Do you know what door this opens?"

I was about to say that I did not know, when I had a chilling thought. I knew even before he told me. The key was to his ex-wife's house. Despite the civil divorce, his ex-wife refused to accept that her marriage was over. She loved Joe, and he was the father of her two children. Joe continued to support his two children and his ex-wife. He was also supporting his new wife and baby. Essentially, he had two families consisting of two wives and three children. The reality was that his first wife had not only become his ex-wife, she had become his mistress. His mistress had become his wife. But he was now cheating on his new wife with his ex-wife. I only had one question.

"Does your new wife know that you are still sleeping with your ex-wife?"

He almost yelled, "Are you crazy?"

Geez, I had to ask.

You can see why a man has absolutely no incentive for his ex-wife and his new wife to be friends. Let me tell you that it is never too late to be friendly with the ex-wife, new girlfriend, new wife, etc.

Here are a few hints if you are the ex-wife:

1. Be compassionate and understanding with the new wife. She needs it.
2. Over margaritas or a bottle of wine, share your stories about him with her.
3. Encourage your ex-husband to involve his new wife in your children's lives.
4. At some point, thank her for taking him off your hands.
5. Count on her to fulfill your ex-husband's obligations to your children.

6. Never talk bad about her.
7. Keep ordering drinks and share more stories about him with her.
8. Remind her that he comes with a "No Return Policy" label.
9. Find at least one thing that you like about the new wife.
10. Remember the new wife's birthday and remember her on Mother's Day. (Chances are, he never will.)

Here are a few hints if you are the new wife:

1. Encourage your husband to be involved in his children's lives and activities.
2. Ask the ex-wife to help you to better understand him.
3. Resist the temptation to mention how good he is to you.
4. Treat her children better than you treat your own.
5. Encourage your husband to maintain his obligations to his children.
6. Never talk bad about her.
7. Never let your husband talk bad about her, especially in front of their children.
8. Make sure he pays his child support on time, and always be generous.
9. Find at least one thing that you like about her.
10. Remember his ex-wife's birthday and remember her on Mother's Day. (Chances are, he never did.)

If there are children involved, try your best to develop an amicable relationship with your husband's ex-wife or with your ex-husband's new wife. Keep the promises that you make to each other, and you will never regret this decision.

14.
Incredible Weight-loss Program

A couple was working in their garden one afternoon.

When the wife bent over to pull some weeds, the husband said, "You're getting fat. Your butt looks huge. I'll bet it's as wide as the gas grill."

After getting a measuring tape, he measured the width of the gas grill, and then he measured his wife's butt.

He then said, "That's what I thought. Your butt and the grill are about the same size."

Feeling hurt and angry, the wife went into the house and didn't speak to her husband the rest of the day.

At bedtime, the husband snuggled up to his wife and nicely said, "Let me show you how much I missed you all day?"

The wife turned her back on her husband, giving him the cold shoulder.

He asked, "What's the matter?"

Without looking at him, the wife said to her husband, "You don't think I'm going to fire up this big-ass grill for one little weenie, do you?"

—Unknown

During our trip to Yellowstone National Park, my husband and I stopped at a convenience store. While he was filling the tank with gas, I went into the store and picked up a few items, including bubble gum, cheese puffs, and a package of chocolate-covered donuts.

As I paid the cashier, she asked me, "Do you need a bag?"

I looked at her and at the woman behind me and said, "Yes. I better hide the cheese puffs and the donuts from my husband."

The cashier and the woman chuckled. Then, the woman said, "I know what you mean. I always hide what I eat from my husband."

I had meant it as a joke. I did not care if my husband saw the cheese puffs or the donuts. Still, it bothered me that this woman felt it was necessary to hide food from her husband. Clearly, she was hiding food from him because he was critical of her weight. She joked about it, but there was a noticeable pain in her voice. I left the store, overcome with sadness for this woman. I silently prayed that her husband would get struck by lightning.

Although I am not overweight, I very well could be. I have always known that if I gain any noticeable weight, my husband will not like it, or allow it.

Even while I was pregnant, I only gained fourteen pounds, and my daughter weighed almost nine pounds. Please understand that I was thirty-seven years old when I had my daughter. I had no business having a baby. Month after month, as the pregnancy progressed, I would look in the mirror and ask myself, "What were you thinking?"

My pregnancy was considered "high risk." I was anemic. I had gestational diabetes, carpal tunnel syndrome, and I completely lost my appetite. I think the loss of appetite was psychosomatic or fear. During my first doctor's visit, I met a woman who said she was in her second trimester. She was about five feet and five inches tall. From the large size of her stomach, it appeared she might be carrying twins. She confided that this was her third baby. She mentioned that she had already gained fifty-six pounds. She knew that her doctor was going to be upset because she had gained eleven pounds since the last visit. A nurse called her name. She gathered her things and walked toward the nurse.

She looked back over her shoulder and said, "Don't be surprised if you gain fifty pounds. You're eating for two, remember?"

I was horrified. I thought, "My husband will leave me if I gain fifty pounds."

Years later, my husband asked me, "Do you now weigh seven pounds more than you did when we got married?"

Without hesitation, I said, "No, do you?"

He did not answer. I did not pursue a response.

A few days later, I asked him, "Why did you ask me if I weighed seven pounds more now than I did when we got married?"

He said, "I was wondering when you were going to come back to that."

He kept me waiting a couple of minutes before he said, "I weigh seven pounds more now than I did when we got married."

I asked him, "Are you sure it isn't more than seven pounds?"

He gave me a dirty look and said, "Seven pounds is your limit. You cannot go above seven pounds."

I asked him what would have happened if he weighed ten or twenty pounds more now than he did when we got married. He said that I should not weigh seven pounds more now than I did when we got married. Talk about validation. I had been dead on all these years. My fear of gaining weight was always present. Still, I was grateful that I was able to maintain my weight all these years.

When I met my friend Terrie, she was battling a weight problem. She was married to Bob, who constantly complained about her weight. She said, "I'm a size 12, but he wants me to be a size 4."

She recalled that when she met Bob, she was a size 8. She acknowledged that nine years and two pregnancies later, she had gained about twenty-five pounds. She had not been able to lose the weight after the children were born.

Bob incessantly teased Terrie about her weight, especially when she was eating. She got to the point where she rarely ate in front of Bob. If he "caught" her eating something, he would poke her in the stomach and ask her, "Do you need to eat that?" Terrie said that Bob would also pinch her around the waist and then show her, with his thumb and index finger, how much he had grabbed. When she would ask him to stop teasing her about her weight, he would tell her that he was only trying to help her lose weight.

Bob would yell at Terrie, "Why can't you lose weight?"

Terrie would cower and ask him, "Why can't you just accept me the way I am?"

Bob also resorted to "helping" Terrie lose weight by calling her names and making oink noises. He enjoyed pushing up the tip of his nose with his finger. This just made him look like the very pig that he was. Bob told Terrie that her physical appearance made it impossible for him to find her sexually attractive. He just had no tolerance for an overweight wife. The level of emotional abuse that he inflicted upon Terrie was unforgivable. It had a detrimental effect on the way Terrie viewed herself. She had no self-esteem. She was unable to accept compliments from anyone, and she put herself down all the time. It was very sad.

On Terrie's birthday one year, she received a one-month pass to a health club from her sister. They agreed to go together. However, when Terrie told Bob about the pass, he told her she had to take the kids. He argued that he was not going to babysit while she was out with her sister at the health club. Since the health club had no babysitting services, Terrie was unable to go. She was so upset with Bob. She felt that, as much as Bob wanted her to lose weight, he set up all the roadblocks.

One day, while she was at work, Terrie got a telephone call from Bob's boss. Bob had been taken to the hospital after experiencing severe chest pains. Terrie rushed to the hospital and found Bob lying on a hospital bed. Bob had to admit to Terrie that the doctor had not only told him that he had high blood pressure, but he was overweight. Bob was instructed to lose at least forty-five pounds over a period of time. Bob was referred to a nutritionist, who could help Bob structure a diet for his weight loss. Bob was also encouraged to begin an exercise program.

Terrie remembered, "I wanted to feel sorry for him, but I could not. All I wanted to do was call him names and laugh in his face. But I did nothing."

Terrie said that Bob held her hand and told her that he needed her to get through this. Terrie knew what that meant.

Since Bob was now officially "sick," he told Terrie that she had to go buy food for his diet plan. Bob expected Terrie to fix his breakfast, pack his lunch, and fix his dinner, according to his diet plan. Bob also told Terrie he needed her encouragement in following his exercise plan. All of this lasted about a week and a half before Bob blamed Terrie for his failure to follow and maintain his diet and exercise programs. He accused her of deliberately sabotaging his attempts. At first, he made feeble attempts to continue his diet and exercise plans. He was consumed with self-pity and anger. The anger, of course, was directed at Terrie. He refused to accept her help. Eventually, he accepted the fact that he, alone, was responsible for his health. However, as he lost weight, he found new ways of badgering Terrie about her weight and her appearance. Understand that only Bob found fault in Terrie's weight and appearance. She was following a diet. She purchased exercise videos, and she was exercising at home. One evening during a huge argument, Bob told Terrie that he could not live with her any longer, and he wanted a separation. Bob left the following weekend.

Terrie said, "It was such a relief after he left. But, I felt so guilty because I never missed him once. All this time, I tried so hard to improve my appearance and lose weight."

I remember telling Terrie, "All you had to do was find out how much Bob weighed. Then you would have known exactly how much weight you needed to lose."

15.

Princess Power

Once upon a time a handsome prince asked a beautiful princess, "Will you marry me?"

The princess thought long and hard. But she said, "No," and she lived happily ever after.

—*Unknown*

Anyone who knows me knows about my club, the Mutual Admiration and Respect Society (MARS). Membership is open only to women. Membership is free and there are no membership dues. Members must promise not to flirt or have sex with their girlfriends' boyfriends or husbands. Members must promise not to backstab their girlfriends, ever. Additionally, members are required to provide unconditional love, encouragement, and emotional support to their girlfriends. To become a member, you have to be a princess. To become a princess, all you have to do is close your eyes, make a wish, and say, "I am a princess."

If anyone has ever called you a princess, I am sure you remember feeling a little giddy. You probably got a smile on your face and felt like you were six years old again. You may have even tilted your head slightly, smiling and feeling special. All my friends will tell you that they are princesses. I can walk into a room of women, and after some simple explanations, every woman there will raise their hands when I say, "Raise your hand if you're a princess."

The rules of the club:

1. Be a great friend to your girlfriends.
2. Provide love, encouragement, and emotional support to your girlfriends.
3. Love to shop. (This is not optional.)
4. Maintain a princess state of mind.

Let me explain the princess state of mind. You have to feel like a princess and behave like a princess. Answer the following questions with, "Because I'm a princess."

1. Why do you need a pedicure?
2. Why do you need a manicure?
3. Why did you buy five new pairs of shoes?
4. Why did you miss work today?
5. Why are you still in your pajamas?
6. Why are you not cooking dinner?
7. Why don't you put gasoline in your car?
8. Why are you in such a good mood?
9. Why do you need a vacation?
10. Why do you need to go shopping?

Additionally, you have to believe that everything in your life has a "princess quality." For example, all snack foods are princess foods: cheese puffs, cheesecake, ice cream, cakes, pies, potato chips, hotdogs, corndogs, pretzels, chocolate-covered donuts, brownies, cookies, and cheese puffs (I love cheese puffs). Recently, I went to a cookout at a local park. I was waiting for a hamburger, and I had asked the cook to warm my hamburger bun. There were other people waiting for hotdogs and hamburgers, including a woman who was right behind me. The cook asked the woman if she needed a hamburger bun. She told him that she wanted a bun, but since she was doing low-carb, she was going bunless. The cook then put my hamburger on my warm bun and put it on my plate.

The woman asked, "How do you do it? You're so thin."

I said, "It's the princess dust."

The woman just stared. I walked away to find a nice place to enjoy my hamburger. The woman walked over to me, with her bunless burger, and said, "Tell me about the princess dust."

First, I told her about MARS. I told her she had to be a princess. I told her that if she was a princess, she got princess dust. She could sprinkle the princess dust to take away the calories from her food. She found all of this amusing.

She said, "I have to go."

I waved to her and said, "Goodbye, Princess."

She said, "I've always wanted to be a princess."

I responded, "Then say it. Say, 'I want to be a princess.'"

She came back and gave me a hug. She left with pockets full of princess dust.

When you are a princess, you sleep in a princess bed with a princess pillow. You wear princess clothes and princess shoes. You drink wine from a princess goblet, and you get a princess hangover. It catches on.

When I was in Alaska, Paul, one of the supervisors where I worked, used to walk down the hallway and greet us as he passed our offices. He would say, "Morning, Tony; morning, Patty; morning, Eric; morning, Princess; morning, Barb; morning, Karen." It was not the same as calling me honey, darling, or sweetheart. It was a state of mind. Even the gifts I received from my friends showed the extent of my princess state of mind. I got T-shirts, coffee mugs, pillows, and plaques that read, "It's Not Easy Being a Princess" and "Princess Power." It is a wonderful thing to feel like a princess. It feels even better to be a member of MARS.

The benefits of membership:

1. You always feel good about yourself.
2. You have a princess support group.

3. You get princess dust. (If you sprinkle it on yourself, you become even more beautiful; if you sprinkle it on your food, it makes calories disappear; if you sprinkle it on your husband, boyfriend, whatever, nothing happens. It doesn't work on men because men are pigs.)

Single or married, every woman needs girlfriends. I have many girlfriends, most of whom I have known for years. I have always been very selective when choosing my girlfriends. I can tell you that they are all honest, loyal, and compassionate. They are strong and supportive. They are generous to a fault. They are bright, intelligent, and beautiful. They all have their own individual sense of humor. They love to laugh. And, of course, they are all princesses! They have brought great joy, hope, and happiness to my life. I love my girlfriends. My life would be so empty without them.

Let me tell you about my relationship with my girlfriends. First, let me say that I have spoiled my girlfriends. Consequently, they all believe they come first in my life, and they do. I could not choose one over another. Therefore, I have chosen to list my girlfriends in alphabetical order. Otherwise, I will never hear the end of it.

<u>Sylvia A.</u>: We met when I was in the eighth grade in 1971. Sylvia was the new girl in school from Chicago. She was sweet and gentle, but she was the toughest girl I had ever known. After she became my friend, no one ever picked on me again. No one I know appreciates music more than she does. Even now, our love of music binds our friendship. For more than thirty years, Sylvia's loyalty and devotion to our friendship has never wavered. We have become women, but we are still just little girls at heart.

<u>Maria Elena B.</u>: Maria Elena is a survivor in so many ways. I do not know if she ever questioned why she was given more challenges than others. If she did, she never complained. Instead, she carried around this incredible strength, and she shared it with others. Along with her physical beauty, her strength makes her beautiful. I remember drawing tornado faces when we were supposed to be listening to the boss. It was so juvenile. Maria Elena taught me that we are never too old to act like kids.

<u>Mary B.</u>: The very first time I spoke to her, I complimented her new Honda Prelude. She responded, "Everything I love is black. My car is black, my dogs are black, my kids are black, and my husband is black." That was it. She walked away.

It was only natural that she and I would become friends. I vividly remember a dinner party at her home. Mary's husband prepared the best filet mignon I had ever had. It was a great party. I remember thinking, "Where are the children?" By the way, her husband is not black and she doesn't have any children.

The turning point in our friendship was when she found out she was going to the law enforcement academy in Georgia. She needed to prepare for the physical part of the training. For several weeks, I made her run up and then down the parking garage (I ran with her). Lisa and I were so proud of her when she graduated from the academy. To this day, I know this is one of her greatest accomplishments.

Mary's visit to Alaska solidified our friendship. She did not complain that it was November, and it was colder than it was in the freezer. She did not complain when we stayed in the remote cabins. She did not complain that we had to urinate in an outhouse. She was in Alaska visiting friends. She was just grateful to be on vacation. I had to work a couple of days while she was visiting. No problem. She got a chance to spend time with my husband. She became a baseball fan during that time.

<u>Karen B.</u>: We became friends because we worked together. She was a terrific supervisor. When I wanted to move from Alaska to the Lower 48, she supported my decision. I loved living in Alaska, I loved my job, and I loved the people I worked with. But, it was time to go and she understood. I still have the pink teddy bears, the blue sweatshirt with the logo "Don't Even Think About a Leash," and the "princess" snow globes she gave me. That's a lot of presents. She spoiled me. I don't know anyone who can say that about a supervisor.

<u>Olga C.</u>: My dear, dear friend. We met thousands of miles from home. We did not find out until later that we only lived seven miles from each other back home.

What didn't she teach me? About the most valuable lesson she taught me was to get along with my husband's ex-wife. I admired the relationship she shared with her ex-husband's wife. I hope more women will embrace this concept. She also taught me about angels and mantras, and how to get what you want in life by asking for it.

Her generosity is legendary. One time, we were driving along a road. I pointed out a beautiful house to her. She looked at the house and asked, "Shall I buy it for you?"

When I said I liked her black and cream-colored striped blouse, she unbuttoned the blouse, took it off, and handed it to me. "It's yours," she said.

I said, "I don't want your blouse. It just looks nice on you."

Incidentally, I love her white leather chaise.

<u>Taryn C.</u>: Taryn is my new little sister and the youngest of my girlfriends. Although I am old enough to be her mother, she never treats me as such. I would like to think it is because I don't look old enough to be her mother. I love that she has fantastic parents, a wonderful sister, and a terrific daughter. She is an excellent mother and a terrific wife. Travis, I don't care what you think. Your wife is a princess. When I brought up the possibility of carpooling with her, she simply said, "Sure." She will never know how much this simplified my life. I want to thank her for taking care of my critter and picking up my mail while I was on vacation. I was not upset that she almost killed my one and only plant. I am so sad that I will miss the entirety of her pregnancy. I promise to return after the birth of the baby.

<u>Carma D.</u>: Carma is a breath of fresh air. She is a princess in every sense of the word. Even her husband, Bruce, knows that she is a princess. He once made a princess bed for her. That is a sign of a good man. She is one of the lucky ones. I am sad that we did not know each other longer. I always looked forward to going to work each morning because she was there. We are lifelong girlfriends. I hope she knows how important she is to me and how much I miss her.

<u>Cherie H.</u>: I am convinced that Princess Destiny brought us together. Our friendship was meant to be. Cherie's mother's name is Sylvia Ann

and her father's name is Kenneth Dean, just like me and my husband. Cherie has been consistently supportive of everything that I do. She truly is an extraordinary friend and a huge inspiration to me. Cherie not only befriended me, she befriended my daughter. My daughter worships her. Everything I know to be true about Cherie I attribute to the fact that she has a wonderful mother. She is truly blessed.

<u>Lena J.</u>: In early 1996, I called and told her that we were moving to Alaska. She sent me her home address. About a week after we arrived in Anchorage, we went to visit her. She was the only person we knew. During our visit, she mentioned that she had an easy work schedule. She asked me to come to her home every morning when my husband came to Anchorage to work. She even told me I was welcome at her home whether she was working or not. She gave me a set of keys to let myself into her home. I was overwhelmed by her generosity, which I knew was entirely sincere. When she left to work in Kotzebue for a week, she let us stay in her home. She let me know, in no uncertain terms, that we were welcome. I did not want to spend my days in a twenty-six-foot travel trailer, in an RV park surrounded by woods, black bears, brown bears, and moose. I made it a point to get up every morning and made my husband take us to her house. It didn't take long for him to express his annoyance. He said that I was going to wear out my welcome.

One day, Lena called and said that she was off the following day. She made me promise to come to Anchorage so we could spend the day together. The next morning, my husband was not pleased at my insistence on going to Lena's house. We arrived at about 6:50 a.m. Lena was already awake and making coffee. She had set out two coffee mugs, along with our favorite coffee creamer. She seemed genuinely excited at our arrival, and we started giggling at nothing. I lost no time telling her that my husband had warned me on the way to her home that I was wearing out my welcome. She simply said, "Kenny's the Devil."

Lena trusted us when she had no reason to. She invited us to her home and let us stay in her home even when she was gone. I marvel at the level of her hospitality. She will never know how grateful I am to her for taking care of us when we moved to Alaska.

<u>Stella L.</u>: When I listen to a George Strait song, I think of Stella. Not just the concert we went to, but the fact that she wanted to put a huge poster of George Strait on her bedroom ceiling. Her husband didn't let her.

Years ago, I had a great visit with her and her family in California. Her parents made me feel so welcome in their home. Her father told me to make myself at home and to get whatever I wanted. Her mother made oatmeal every morning. I remember that Stella's kids could say the word "mom" so many times in a row it sounded like they were trying to start a car. I hope they don't do that anymore.

<u>Cindy M.</u>: From the beginning of our friendship, we had a "heart-to-heart" talk. We promised each other that our friendship would be based on trust. We have never faltered. My life has become entwined with hers. Her father and sisters accepted me from the beginning. Her mother, I hoped, would come around. I remember the day that her mother thanked me for being such a good friend to her daughter. She had accepted me because she knew that her daughter and I were truly friends. I had earned her trust and respect. I will always cherish that memory. Cindy and I have shared some wonderful times together. I miss the parties she had at her home. I think we were in our thirties when we finally grew up. Now, we have kids. We even managed to have children at the same time. They are only nine months apart. Now, they will grow up together.

As I struggled to complete this book, Cindy gave me a key to her home and granted me full access. She gave me things I didn't know I needed. I am forever in her debt.

<u>Lisa M.</u>: Lisa and I met through a mutual friend, Wally. We were instantly drawn to each other. Months later, we learned we share the same birth date, June 15. That explained everything. She possesses all of the ideals that I believe in. She is empathic and genuine with others. She is trustworthy and loyal. She is so beautiful, and she makes it so easy to be around her. We're getting used to being the only two laughing at something that nobody else finds amusing.

<u>Elizabeth (Lisa) L. S.</u>: With the exception of the weekends, for years Lisa and I spent almost every morning drinking coffee together. After I moved to Alaska, one of the things that I missed most was having coffee with Lisa.

When I was pregnant, she brought me some of her maternity clothes. She shared her birthing experience (without frightening me). She also planned the greatest baby shower ever. It is no wonder that I named my daughter after her.

I remember that when we were going to college, we would split our lunches, which we brought from home. Lunch was usually one baloney sandwich, one peanut butter and jelly sandwich, and one bag of chips. On campus, we bought one can of soda, and we split that, too. We were so broke all the time. We were lucky if we had five dollars for gas. Look at us now. If we eat a baloney sandwich, it's by choice. I am so proud of her accomplishments. She has succeeded and surpassed others in an almost strictly male-dominated field. Nanner, nanner, boo, boo!

<u>Sonia G. S.</u>: Sonia is the one person I know who loves to shop ten times more than I do. That is only because she, I mean, her husband can afford it. She has the most beautiful clothes and shoes. She should think about opening her own boutique. Someday, when she is not looking, I am going to raid her closet and take everything I want. I know she won't mind. She will just go buy new stuff.

One of the things that I adore about her is that she can totally be herself with me. I remember that I once called her cellular telephone. When she answered the telephone, I asked her, "Where are you?" She said, "I'm getting my nails done so I can be even more beautiful." That she is!

Sonia did something for me once, which prompted me to tell her, "Now, you are my best friend." She came to my house and brought me about ten dozen homemade tamales, which she and her sister had spent all day making. All day! Here she was, a doctor's wife and a princess, of course, making tamales just for me. This was about a week after she drove to San Antonio with her two daughters and her sister solely to visit my father and me while we were in the hospital. I love her so much for that.

<u>Sandra V.</u>: Sandra possesses such a quiet gentleness. I find it incredibly soothing to be around her. She always makes me feel that I am her best friend and the most important person in her life. She has shared some of the most important events in my life. I still have the huge white and pink giraffe she gave me when Lisa was born.

She has been a great friend to me. Every time I came home to visit, I saw her more than I did any of the rest of my friends. Sandra made it a priority to spend as much time as possible with us during our visit. She made herself available to take us shopping, to run errands, and to take us anywhere we needed to go. We always have so much fun together. I have to thank Tony for being so understanding.

<u>Maria L. W.</u>: I still remember the day she came to look at the condominium upstairs from me. I knew that we were going to be friends forever. We are a testament to the kind of relationship all tenants and landlords should share. She has surpassed her own expectations. I remember when she was taking her first college English course. She was terrified. But together, we got through the semester, working every evening when we could have been playing. When the semester was over, she came over to tell me that she had gotten her grades. She was so excited when she screamed, "We got an A!" I am so proud of her. She is a wonderful friend. Whenever I had to go to the airport (usually late at night), she always took care of my daughter. I can still picture her dragging her blanket and pillow downstairs. We have had so much fun together. We have laughed until we cried. She blesses my life. She always makes me believe that I can be a better person.

There is nothing better than the gift of friendship. It is a wonderful thing to give and an even more wonderful thing to accept. We need our girlfriends. With the exception of our families, our girlfriends are the only constant in our lives. More often than not, we depend on our girlfriends instead of our husbands or boyfriends. We know that our friendships with our girlfriends are solid. Still, we strive to achieve great relationships with our husbands or boyfriends. That takes greater effort.

16.
I Once Discovered the Secret to a Perfect Marriage, but I Forgot to Write It Down

A man was sitting on the couch watching television when his wife came up behind him and hit him on the head with a frying pan.

He said, "What was that for?"

She said, "I found that piece of paper in your pants with the name Betty Sue written on it."

The man explained, "I went to the races last week. Betty Sue was the name of one of the horses I bet on."

The wife apologized to her husband.

A few days later, the wife came up behind her husband and hit him again on the head with a frying pan.

When he came to, he asked her, "What was that for?"

She replied, "Your horse just called."

—Unknown

When we are in a terrific relationship, we have a high expectation for a harmonious and happy marriage. However, during the course of these relationships and marriages, many women find that their most basic emotional needs, such as love, affection, trust, honesty, respect, communication, and financial support, are not being met. We want men to show us love and affection, without wanting sex. We want men to be truthful and honest with us, without being brutally honest. We want men to appreciate us and to take an interest in what we do, without wanting sex. We want to be able to have a conversation, without having to wait for a commercial. We want to be taken care of, without being taken advantage of. We especially want men to love and accept the way we are and the way we look, without exception. Raise your hand if all of your emotional needs are being met. Zero, huh? Let's try again. Raise your hand if one of your emotional needs is being met. Yes, most of us fall into this category.

An easy test to determine if there is any love left in a marriage is to try to find a greeting card for your husband for an important occasion: birthday, anniversary, Father's Day, job promotion. You've seen these cards. The front side of the cards read, "Hugs and Kisses on Your Birthday," or "To a Wonderful Husband on Our Anniversary," or "For a Special Husband on Father's Day." If you put all of these cards back because he is not so wonderful or special, and you would rather hug and kiss someone else, the love is probably gone. If your husband gets a job promotion and the only card you like reads, "Congratulations! It's Funny How Shit Rises to the Top," then, the love is definitely gone.

If you are in a relationship, but you are not married, you can end the relationship for any reason at any time. Period! While there are a number of reasons to end a marriage, not all of them are good reasons. There are only two very good reasons to consider ending a marriage: abuse and deception.

Abuse, whether it is physical, sexual, verbal, or emotional, always escalates with time. Always! The list of abusive behavior is endless. No one should ever have to suffer or endure any type of abuse in any relationship. Often the abuse begins during dating and continues well into the marriage. You have every right, and certainly every reason, to end a marriage if he physically abuses you in any manner; if he forces you or manipulates you into unwanted sexual activity; if he consistently calls you names, which hurt you or humiliate you; if he threatens you or someone you love with physical harm; or if he is excessively controlling. However, more often than not, the decision to leave is very difficult.

My friend Dawn was a victim of physical and verbal abuse at the hands of her husband, Jerry. At first, she denied the abuse. Later, she just stayed away from her friends and family. One night, my husband answered a knock on the door and found Dawn badly beaten and very bloody. He helped Dawn walk to my bedroom. The way he looked at Dawn, I could see he was shaken by her appearance. Dawn was bleeding so much that it was difficult to determine exactly where her injuries were located. I tried, in vain, to talk her into going to the hospital. She assured me that it looked worse than it was. I helped her undress in my bathroom and cleaned up her cuts. She had a cut on her forehead, cuts over and under her left eye, cuts on her upper and lower lip, and a bloody nose. Most of her fingernails were torn off. She had abrasions on her knees and on the tops of her feet and toes. Apparently, after Jerry beat her, he pulled Dawn out of the house. Then, he dragged her on the ground out to the street. Dawn said she stayed there until she felt strong enough to get up. From there, she walked to my house. Incidentally, Jerry had beaten Dawn because he found soapsuds on the dishes she had just washed and rinsed.

As I cleaned her cuts, I fought back the temptation to ask her why she stayed with Jerry. Sensing my thoughts, Dawn said, "I know I should leave him. But, I can't. He's threatened to kill me and to kill my family. I'm afraid he'll take the kids and never bring them back."

I tried not to say anything. After I cleaned her up, all I could do was hold her. Dawn said, "Even if I leave, I have nowhere to go. I don't have the money to rent an apartment. I can't afford to leave." Then, she said, "I still love him in my own way."

I knew there was nothing I could do. Within hours, Dawn was ready to go home. She thanked me for taking care of her. I dropped her off at home and gave her some money. I told her I would always help her, and when she was ready, I would help her plan her escape. She nodded and walked away.

About two years later, I ran into Dawn at the mall. She wasn't married to Jerry anymore. She said that Jerry had left her after he found a new girlfriend. Dawn said, "But he didn't leave for good right away. He kept coming over to see us. He didn't tell his girlfriend, but she found out. When Jerry's girlfriend got pregnant, Jerry took it like a man and ran to his mother's house. One day, Jerry's girlfriend came looking for him at my house. I told her he was living with his mother. I noticed that she had bruises on her arms and face, and she was very pregnant. I felt so sorry for her. I felt sorry for me, too. That was the turning point in my life. I took the kids to Virginia and moved in with my brother and his wife. Jerry was furious, but he couldn't hurt me anymore. Now, I'm alone but I'm happy."

I hugged Dawn and wished her luck. We said our goodbyes. I was so relieved that she was no longer with her abusive husband.

Women stay in abusive relationships for a number of reasons, including fear, lack of resources, love, and guilt. Before a woman leaves for good, she has left the relationship three to four times. Each time, she returns. However, the abuse resumes and escalates and she leaves again, if she can walk and if she's still alive. The first thing a woman needs to do to leave an abusive marriage is to make the final decision to leave and not come back. Once the decision is made, it is important to establish a plan. It is equally important to confide in at least one person who is trustworthy and helpful. If it is financially impossible to leave immediately, start saving money and hide it. Look for another place to live or, if possible, ask friends or relatives to provide shelter, temporarily. Be ready to move at a moment's notice. The best time to leave is when he is out of the house. Next, file for divorce. If you don't know a good attorney, contact a women's advocacy group. Ask if they have an attorney referral service. If he is still contacting and harassing you, file a report with the local police department (after every incident) and seek a protective order. Unless it is absolutely necessary, stop all contact with him. If I make it sound easy, I apologize. It isn't easy to leave. However, the alternative could prove to be fatal.

Deception in a marriage is the other reason to contemplate ending a marriage. Deception comes in many forms. A man who lies about the number of times he has been married, the number of children he has, his criminal history, his financial situation, or his addiction to drugs and/or alcohol will only continue to lie. This is how he lives his life. He lies and cheats at will. He has affairs. He finds reasons not to work. He has a hard time keeping a job, or he gets "hurt" at work. He abuses drugs and/or alcohol. He repeatedly goes to jail and/or prison. He opens bank accounts or obtains credit. He ruins your credit and eventually forces you into bankruptcy. It is also not uncommon for him to have and maintain a secret life over the course of the marriage.

Years ago, I met a woman named Beth at a health club. We were in the same kick-boxing class. We usually talked before and after class and always partnered up during class. One day after class, she asked me if I wanted to get a cup of coffee. I jumped at the chance. Over iced vanilla lattes, Beth revealed that she was getting divorced, and she was seeking an annulment.

She said, "I thought I had the best marriage in the world. I had a loving husband, who was wonderful in every way. When I met Richard, his father owned a movie theater. Richard ran the projector, and he worked most evenings. By the time Richard and I got married, Richard's father was showing only adult films at the movie theater. It was much more lucrative. About three years into our marriage, I started to suspect that Richard was having an affair. There were little things that kept adding up. For example, I found cigarette butts in Richard's car, but he didn't smoke. He also didn't have any friends who smoked. When I asked Richard about the cigarette butts, he explained that his friend Lucas was a smoker. It was the first time I had ever heard he had a friend named Lucas.

"When I told Richard that I had not met Lucas, Richard said he would ask him to come by. Lucas started coming over on the weekends.

His story was that he was getting over a breakup. I offered to set him up with one of my friends, but he wasn't interested in a new relationship."

Beth lowered her voice and continued, "Richard started coming home very late. When I asked him where he was, he said he was at the movie theater. However, when I called there, he would not answer the telephone. Late one night, I drove over to the movie theater and parked my car around the block. I found a spot across from the movie theater and hid in the shadows. About an hour later, I saw Richard and Lucas walking out of the movie theater. As Richard locked the doors, I saw Lucas reach behind Richard and hug him. Richard turned around and kissed Lucas on the mouth. I could not believe what I was seeing. Richard walked with Lucas to the parking lot, where their cars were parked. Before Richard got into his car, he and Lucas exchanged a long kiss. I couldn't believe it, but there was no mistaking what I was seeing. I couldn't move. I saw Richard drive away. I thought about running to my car and catching up with Richard. Instead, I stepped out of the shadows so that Lucas could see me. He was neither shocked nor surprised to see me. I walked over to Lucas and asked him what was going on.

"Lucas told me, 'He loves me, but you're in the way.' I started crying. I couldn't help it. Lucas got into his car. Before he closed the car door, he said, 'Richard has always been like this, even before he married you.'"

As we sat in the coffee shop, Beth looked around to see if anyone could hear her. Then she continued, "When I got home, Richard was sitting at the kitchen table waiting for me. Lucas had called and warned him that I knew. I didn't ask Richard anything. I didn't know what to ask. I felt numb. I couldn't pull one thought together. Richard stood and walked over to me. He hugged me and said, 'I do love you, but not like that. I'm sorry.' I went through many emotions during that time. I was angry and hurt, and I was so confused. I never suspected that Richard was gay. In the end, I had to let Richard go. The hardest part was explaining to my family why Richard and I were getting a divorce."

Beth and I finished our coffee and promised to do this again. As we walked out of the coffee shop, Beth said, "It is hard enough to lose a man to another woman. But to lose him to another man is more than devastating."

I continued to see Beth at the health club. However, after a few weeks, Beth stopped coming to class. I never saw her again.

Seeking a divorce because the marriage has an element of fraud is more than acceptable. In fact, the marriage can be annulled. However, every state has different requirements as to the nature of the deception that was committed.

Before couples end their marriages, they sometimes consider marriage counseling. That is great, if you want to try to save your marriage. As for me, I could not imagine asking my husband to go to a marriage counselor. I can't even get him to go to the mall. I do not know a single person or couple that ever said that marriage counseling saved their marriage. I'm sure it does happen. Make no mistake, I am not blaming the counselor or saying that counseling cannot be effective. The fact of the matter is that people who seek the help of a marriage counselor often fail to follow the advice of the counselor. Think of all the times you went to the doctor. When did you quit taking the prescribed medication? You quit taking it as soon as you felt better, didn't you? Counseling can have the same effect. After a few sessions, the relationship may appear to be getting better. Some changes may occur overnight, and the marriage may even appear to be better than ever. When you are involved in an abusive relationship or in a relationship based on deception and lies, you know, through experience, that he will not change. He rather quickly reverts to the behavior he has learned to embrace.

You do not have to be stuck in a bad marriage. You do not have to be miserable. Sometimes divorce is necessary. However, divorce lawyers can be quite expensive. It might be cheaper to hire a hit man. Then you keep everything! However, there are serious risks involved here, like your freedom. Remember that freedom is what you wanted in the first place. As I was saying, divorce lawyers can be quite expensive. In the long run, a good lawyer is cheaper than a bad husband.

What about the rest of us? Well, I don't know about you, but I'm not leaving my husband. He isn't perfect, but he tries his best. Besides, I truly love my husband, quirks and all. I work at my relationship with my husband. I pick my battles. The rest, I just let it go. There are two pieces of advice I can give you if you are staying in your relationship "for better or for worse."

1. Lower your expectations.
2. If your expectations are already very low, then don't have any. If you have no expectations, you cannot be disappointed.

Whatever you do, don't wake up one day with him lying next to you and think, "Oh no, he's still here and my life is just about over." We only get one shot at this. Find what truly makes you happy. Make everything fun. Love and live like there's no tomorrow.

About the Author

Sylvia Carvajal was born in Corpus Christi, Texas, in 1958. She grew up in the Rio Grande Valley in South Texas. After graduating from high school, she served three years in the military. In 1986, she earned a degree in sociology, with a minor in criminal justice. She then worked as a U.S. Probation and Pretrial Services Officer for fourteen years. She has lived in Germany, Alaska, California, and Idaho. She resides in South Texas with her husband and daughter. She is currently at work on a second book.

Printed in the United States
61450LVS00002B/205-498